PRESENTED TO:

FROM:

DATE:

Baking

WITH

The Bread Lady

DELICIOUSNESS YOU CAN MASTER AT HOME

SARAH GONZALEZ

 ZONDERVAN®

ZONDERVAN

Baking with The Bread Lady
Copyright © 2021 by Sarah Gonzalez

Requests for information should be addressed to:
Zondervan, *3900 Sparks Dr. SE, Grand Rapids, Michigan 49546*

ISBN 978-0-310-5827-2 (hardcover)
ISBN 978-0-310-45829-6 (audio)
ISBN 978-0-310-5826-5 (ebook)

Art direction and cover design: Tiffany Forester
Photography: Sarah Gonzalez
Additional photography: Katie Thomas (pages viii and 252)
Interior Design: Emily Ghattas

Printed in China
21 22 23 24 25 GRI 10 9 8 7 6 5 4 3 2 1

To Corey and Eva.

Contents

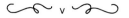

CAKES AND FROSTINGS 125

Frostings, Icings, and Fillings . . 158

COOKIES AND BARS . . 173

GF = Gluten-Free Recipes

Introduction

They broke bread in their homes and ate together with glad and sincere hearts.

ACTS 2:46

When I began my little bread business six years ago, I never thought it would turn into a full-fledged bakery. I just knew I wanted to feed people and inspire them to cook and bake. After moving to Spring Hill, Tennessee, a town of transplants, I learned that everyone was homesick for somewhere, yearning for a sense of belonging and the comforts of home. The one thing that connected many of us was comfort food made by our mothers or grandmothers. Heartwarming edible nostalgia that filled not only our tummies but, more importantly, our souls. I decided I was going to do my best to fulfill that role for our community and become the town's surrogate grandmother, even though I was only in my early thirties. I wanted to bring people together and welcome them to take a seat at my table, and thus Spring Hill Bakery was born.

I started out on a shoestring budget, showing up to my first farmers' market with a folding table, a blue plastic tablecloth, and my first logo I hand-painted on a giant wooden pizza peel. Humble beginnings. I'd announced on our community Facebook page that I was starting a small business selling bread, not knowing what to expect. I wasn't sure if Spring Hill even had a bakery. To my surprise, I sold out quickly that first week at the farmers' market. Each week the line to my booth grew longer and longer. I realized I might actually have a real business.

In the first year, I'd gone from selling goods out of the trunk of my car in a parking lot to my first commercial kitchen in a haunted mansion. I'd baked for events at the Tennessee Governor's Mansion, opened wholesale accounts with local restaurants, and gained more and more local support. It was unbelievable, especially considering I had never worked in food service before. I was armed only with what I'd learned from family and from my own experimenting.

Growing up, everyone cooked and baked—my gramma, my mom, my aunts, my cousins, and several generations before that. I guess you could say it was in our blood. Every family event was centered around food. Holidays, fruit-picking parties in Aunt Teena's backyard, and canning days at Gramma's. Some of my earliest memories are of standing on a chair or stool to help with meals, stirring this or peeling that, setting the table, and sitting on the floor in front of the oven, peering inside to watch what that magic box could do.

I was hooked.

Customers began calling me the Bread Lady, and soon I answered to that more often than my own name.

Thus began my lifelong love affair with food—starting with what my parents refer to as my "spaghetti phase," when, anytime I cooked, they knew it was pasta for dinner *again* as I fine-tuned recipes. It amazed me how just a few tweaks could change food so much. It was like mad science you could eat. Then there were the chocolate chip cookies that tasted so good when coffee was added—a trick I'd learned from obsessively watching Ina Garten. I decided they couldn't possibly be better . . . until the next time I made them. The exploration was endless.

Years later my booth at the big farmers' market became an opportunity to test new creations. I came up with new breads and meal ideas for customers to try. I made videos showing how to create an amazing steak sandwich on the Cuban loaves that would be available that week. Other videos demonstrated how to make French toast and bread pudding in order to use up bread that had gone stale. I shared tips on entertaining and meal prep with the hope that others would capture the vision of breaking bread and feeding others too. Customers began calling me the Bread Lady, and soon I answered to that more often than my own name.

After three years and eleven months of searching for the ideal place where I could feed people at my own table, I opened Spring Hill Bakery as a brick and mortar. After what felt like forty years of wandering, I could finally provide a place in our community to gather and break bread, making our ever-growing city still feel like a small town. At the bakery we made everything from scratch like our grandmothers had and transformed the front to feel like you were visiting Grandma herself. In the beginning, the bakery was everything I'd dreamed it could be.

After eighteen months of unbelievable success, awards, television appearances, and a regular line that wrapped around our 925-square-foot building, I made the decision to shut the doors on the bakery because the work and stress had almost consumed me. I was no longer focused on the mission—breaking bread together and teaching people to fall in love with baking for each other. Now I was just trying to make it through the week, sometimes just getting through the day. I didn't like where we were headed or who I was becoming, so I got off the track that was taking me further and further away from the reason I had started in the first place.

This cookbook is a collection of baking recipes comprised of family secrets enjoyed regularly at our table. You'll find unearthed treasures from my great-grandmother that would have otherwise been long forgotten and creations I've come up with myself, many of which were lovingly made and served at my bakery. This collection is filled with stories of family, togetherness, and love. Perhaps stories similar to your own. You'll read the secrets to my cinnamon rolls, which were made by the hundreds every morning; my gramma's molasses cookies, which taste like every happy Christmas memory; and even the bread made and donated to some of my local churches to be used in the ultimate act of breaking bread: Communion.

This cookbook is also an invitation. To invite you not only to bake this deliciousness for yourself and your own family but also to bake these cherished recipes for others. Continue the tradition of breaking bread with people in your own

> You'll find unearthed treasures from my great-grandmother that would have otherwise been long forgotten and creations I've come up with myself, many of which were lovingly made and served at my bakery.

communities. By the time this book finds its way to you, I don't know where the state of the world will be. As these recipes and stories have been compiled and written, we're still in the thick of a pandemic that has separated friends from friends and family from family. My hope is that as the world heals, we remember to come back together again and serve one another at our tables. Welcome new neighbors with warmth and sustenance, create new memories that will someday be triggered by the perfect blend of sugar and butter, and feed one another—hearts, bellies, and souls.

The Care and Eating of Bread

Taking care of a loaf of bread seems easy enough. You buy it, bring it home, maybe put it in the pantry or perhaps even the fridge. Some leave it on the counter, and others store it in the microwave. But what is the right way to store bread? *Is* there a right way?

While store-bought bread and homemade bread are similar, there are some surprising differences above and beyond flavor and appearance. Homemade bread has a fraction of the ingredients as store-bought bread, which means there aren't any hard-to-pronounce preservatives. No preservatives means it's healthier. It also means that it has a much shorter shelf life than anything you'll find in the bread aisle. Since most homemade breads typically last only a few days sitting out on the counter, there are ways to preserve and store your bread to make it last longer and allow it to stale or dry instead of growing mold. The same cannot be said for moldy bread. No one enjoys discovering a "science project" when all they want is a sandwich!

Storing Bread: The best place to store bread is in a paper bag kept in a bread box. This allows for your bread to be vented properly so it won't mold. Store your bread box in a cool, dry place. Large appliances like dishwashers and refrigerators radiate heat, which can speed up the molding process and dry out your bread faster.

Refrigerating your bread is also a big no-no because it too will dry out bread super quickly. Freezing, on the other hand, is perfectly fine—provided the bread is wrapped tightly in a sealed bag. It's best to use the bread within a few months for optimum taste and texture.

Thawing Bread: Thawing frozen bread is pretty easy if you plan ahead. Take it out of the freezer, unwrap it so the condensation doesn't make for soggy bread, and allow it to come to room temperature.

If you're planning on using the entire loaf, you can bake it at 325 for about 30 minutes or until it's warm all the way through. If you're thawing sliced bread for toast, you can simply pop a frozen slice straight into your toaster.

Reheating bread: If you've just made a loaf of bread and you'd like to reheat it whole, bake at 350 for about 15–20 minutes or until it's warm and the crust is crunchy. Give it a little squeeze to hear it crackle.

Please, whatever you do, do not microwave your bread. If you've ever done it, you know that it'll be really soft at first, but then as it cools, it hardens into something resembling rawhide. That's because one of the sugar molecules in the wheat starch liquefies during heating and crystalizes as it cools. It negatively affects not only the texture, but the flavor too.

Remember: microwave use is bread abuse.

Toasting: There are a few methods for toasting bread. Obviously, tossing a few slices in the toaster is the simplest way, but I find I prefer other methods that provide much more taste.

If I'm toasting a few slices, I brush both sides with butter and brown them in a skillet on the stove. The caramelization and crunch are completely divine. For larger crowds, spread the slices on a sheet plan and brush with butter. If you're serving it with a savory meal, large flake salt and fresh cracked pepper are great sprinkled over the top. Then place under a hot broiler for a few minutes until all the slices are browned. You can flip them and repeat the process of you want them toasted on both sides. Just remember to keep a close eye on them because they can go from golden brown to burnt within seconds. Heartbreaking.

Using up leftover or stale bread: Sometimes we forget about that loaf and it gets too hard too quickly. I've done it a lot. If you're stretching a budget or you just hate wasting food, you'll be happy to know that you have options. I've included recipes like French toast, strata, bread pudding, and a Brown Betty that are perfect for dry bread. Since all of these recipes call for some sort of custard or berry juice, the dry bread will soak up all that goodness creating creamy, toasty textures *and* be easy on the wallet.

Pantry Staples

A well-stocked pantry makes it possible to bake whenever you're in need or simply in the mood. These are a few of the ingredients I make sure to keep on hand as well as some information as to why I've chosen certain types of ingredients over others. Most professional chefs and bakers are extra particular about what goes into their food, even if it breaks with what's more widely accepted in the food world. I am no exception.

Flour: The main two flours you will find in this book are all-purpose and bread flour. I tend to use King Arthur, White Lily, or Gold Medal as a standard, however, that shouldn't stop you from baking if you prefer another brand. All-purpose is great for . . . well . . . all purposes. However, to get that chew from a really great bread—especially the cinnamon roll recipes—you will want to make sure you have bread flour on hand as well.

Butter: Every recipe in this book—even the cakes and frostings—call for salted butter. No, that's not a mistake. I've found that many baked goods lack enough salt to really bring out the flavor, so salted butter actually enhances the flavor in an interesting way. You'll find this with the Classic Sugar Cookie recipe where the flavor is meant to be more salty-sweet than just sweet. Purists may call it sacrilegious;

I call it a flavor adventure. If you are a seasoned baker and cannot bear the thought of using salted butter, by all means, use what you love.

Salt: Whether you use Diamond Crystal or Morton's, coarse kosher salt is vital. It's more flaky than normal table salt and allows you to salt more gradually. Using table salt will make everything way too salty. When sea salt is called for, something really flaky like Maldon is preferred.

Yeast: Red Star active dry yeast has been my go-to for years. Some recipes call for proofing or blooming before beginning your recipe, but I find that isn't always necessary. In some recipes, it can be added in with the flour and will activate just fine during the initial rise, provided your water is at the right temperature.

I like to buy my yeast in a two-pound block available online or at restaurant supply stores, and store most of it in the freezer. Then I can fill my smaller container and store it in the refrigerator. This way it can keep for months without going bad and it's far more economical to buy in bulk.

Sugar: Aside from the expected granulated and confectioner's sugars, I do keep a few specific kinds on hand. The first is dark brown sugar. The darker the sugar, the more molasses it contains. This means the sugar is going to have a deep, rich flavor that will add more than just sweetness to your recipes. In the chance that you have only golden brown, you can add a tablespoon of molasses to make up the difference.

The second is turbinado. When I need a thicker granule of sugar for sprinkling a piecrust, I like to use turbinado instead of a sanding sugar if it doesn't need to be pure white. It has a slight brown sugar flavor and is light tan in color, so it will change the color of frostings and other light-colored baked goods.

Shortening: Some recipes call for a bit of shortening. To add a more complex flavor, I always substitute butter-flavored shortening in place of plain. You will see the biggest difference in the piecrust recipe, but it does make quite a difference in the others as well.

Milk: Whether a recipe calls for regular milk or buttermilk, I always use full fat when it comes to baking. I find that the flavor and texture is better than when I use a lower fat dairy. The same applies for yogurt or sour cream. It just takes it to the next level and anything that can taste more like Gramma made it, that's the version I want to experience.

These are just the basics that I always keep on hand. Aside from eggs and soda leavening, you can make a ton of different items with just these pantry staples. To make sure I'm not using expired ingredients, I always boldly mark my ingredients with the expiration date so I can see at a glance what I need to use up.

Now let's get baking!

Equipment

When it comes to baking, there are quite a lot of tools that you'll need in your arsenal. Luckily there is a lot of crossover into cooking, so you may already have many of these. There are, however, some tools that I absolutely cannot bake without and it is these tools that make baking that much easier.

Food scale: Whether you're weighing ingredients or weighing dough, this tool is imperative for consistency. Some of the recipes call for cutting the dough into equal parts. This will ensure the pretzels, rolls, or loaves are the same size, which will ensure that they bake evenly.

Bowl scraper: Made of flexible plastic, this tool does more than effectively clean out bowls. I also use it to spread things like cinnamon filling and hazelnut spread more evenly over dough. It provides a lot more control than a handled scraper and covers a lot more area. While I have scrapers of all types, this is one I definitely cannot bake without.

Bench scraper: Unlike the bowl scraper, this tool is made of metal and either has a curved handle or one made of wood. This tool is great at efficiently picking up and moving rested dough, as well as sectioning biscuits and cutting bread dough into smaller pieces. The trick is to cut straight down in a chopping motion instead of trying to slice. It also makes an excellent tool for chilling cold butter and even clearing your work surface of flour and stuck-on ingredients before wiping everything down.

Immersion blender: Also called a *stick blender*, this tool is great for whisking lots of eggs at once. There are also models that come with additional attachments like a mini food processor and a whisk to take care of small jobs like chopping nuts, crushing graham crackers, and creating foam.

Dough whisk: Different from a balloon whisk, a dough whisk is made of a thick, ridged metal meant for blending dough by hand. The handle end of a wooden spoon can also be used, however I find that a dough whisk is much more efficient.

Mixers: Aside from a stand mixer—which is an invaluable tool—I also have occasion to use an electric hand mixer. One such use is creating perhaps my favorite recipe in this book, the Smoky Seven Minute Frosting (see page 163), which is made over a double boiler, or a heat-safe bowl that fits safely on a sauce pan.

Cake and loaf pans: There are various cake and loaf pans used in this book. Here is a list of all the different kinds that are used throughout the book. Some recipes give you options to bake in different sizes, so all are not necessary. Keep in mind that metal will bake more quickly than glass and create a crispier crust on bread loaves.

Additionally, you will need measuring cups and spoons, extra mixing bowls, whisks, a cooling rack, and a sifter or sieve. For cakes, you may need a piping bag and tips, offset spatulas, and a plethora of other tools, however this will depend on your particular baking needs. You can bake a lot of beautiful things without a lot of tools!

9x13

8x4 loaf

9x5 loaf

8x8 square

9x9 square

6-inch round

8-inch round

9-inch round

9-inch pie

9-inch tart

10-cup bundt pan

13x18-inch sheet pan (cookie sheet)

Breads

Quick Breads

Quick breads are a great place to start making bread if you're a beginner, but they're also one of my favorite go-tos as they are . . . well . . . quick. Quick breads are made with a leavening agent, such as baking powder or baking soda, that rises more quickly and requires no leavening period before baking so that it can be baked as soon as the dough is made.

Lemon Blueberry Bread

Fresh blueberries and lemons celebrate summer perfectly in this bread!
A bakery favorite, this moist and buttery loaf is packed with lemon
flavor, even in the icing drizzled over the top. Frozen blueberries can be
used, but increase the baking time by approximately ten minutes.

BREAD INGREDIENTS

1 cup white sugar

3/4 cup (1 1/2 sticks) salted
butter, melted

2 large eggs

1/4 cup fresh lemon juice

1 tablespoon fresh lemon zest

1 1/2 cups plus 1 tablespoon
all-purpose flour, divided

1 teaspoon baking powder

1 teaspoon kosher salt

1/2 cup whole milk

1 cup fresh blueberries

ICING INGREDIENTS

1 cup powdered sugar

2 to 3 tablespoons lemon juice

1 teaspoon lemon zest

Yield: one 8 x 4-inch loaf

Prep time: 10 minutes

Bake time: 1 hour

DIRECTIONS

1. Preheat oven to 350 degrees.

2. In the bowl of an electric mixer fitted with the
paddle attachment, mix together sugar and
melted butter. Add in eggs and mix on medium
until light and fluffy. Add lemon juice and zest,
and mix until fully combined.

3. In a separate bowl whisk together flour, baking
powder, and salt. Add to egg mixture alternately
with the milk and mix until just combined.
Batter can still be lumpy, but texture should be
consistent throughout.

4. Toss rinsed fresh blueberries in 1 tablespoon
of flour. Carefully fold blueberries into batter
without breaking them. Pour batter into greased
loaf pan and bake for 60 minutes or until
toothpick comes out clean.

5. Cool for 1 hour before removing from pan to
cooling rack. Allow to cool completely before
glazing.

6. To make icing, in a small bowl whisk together
powdered sugar, lemon juice, and lemon zest.
Consistency should be thick enough that it
doesn't run clear when drizzled over your
finger. Drizzle loaf with glaze and allow to set
completely.

The Best Banana Bread

Greek yogurt is the secret behind this incredibly moist loaf of banana bread. The tartness of the yogurt adds so much flavor, making this a sure family favorite. Sour cream or a flavored yogurt works well too. Substituting a flavored Greek yogurt, like strawberry or peach, is a super simple way to change up the flavor and create interesting combinations.

INGREDIENTS

2 cups all-purpose flour

3/4 teaspoon baking soda

1 teaspoon kosher salt

1 cup white sugar

1/2 cup (1 stick) butter, softened

2 large eggs

2 teaspoons vanilla extract

3 very ripe bananas, mashed

1/3 cup Greek yogurt

DIRECTIONS

1. Preheat oven to 350 degrees.

2. Combine flour, baking soda, and salt in a bowl, stirring with a whisk.

3. In the bowl of an electric mixer fitted with the paddle attachment, cream together sugar and butter, beating until light and fluffy. Scrape down sides of the bowl. Add eggs one at a time, beating well after each addition. Add vanilla, banana, and yogurt, and combine.

4. Add flour mixture and stir just until it fully comes together.

5. Pour batter into a greased loaf pan. Bake for 1 hour, or until a toothpick comes out clean. Loaf should have a crack along the top ridge. Allow to cool in the pan for 10 minutes, then remove from pan and allow to cool completely on a cooling rack.

Yield: one 9 x 5-inch loaf

Prep time: 10 minutes

Bake time: 60 minutes

The Care and Feeding of Neighbors

Are they moving away already?" I asked my husband, Corey, noticing the sign in our neighbors' front yard. It felt like they had just moved in a few months ago.

We continued on our morning walk, and I began to think of all the families who had moved in and out of our subdivision since we migrated to Tennessee seven years before. Having moved from the West Coast to a place where we knew exactly two people, it always crossed my mind that the new families might be in the exact same situation.

Moving can be tough for the first few weeks as belongings get unpacked, surroundings become slightly more familiar, and friendships slowly start to form. Learning to navigate a new town and even adjusting to a new culture can be jarring and make a person feel homesick.

I thought back to that mid-October day when we first pulled into the driveway of our new suburban brick-front house, two thousand miles away from stucco and palm trees. Corey and I were both excited and terrified for the great unknown in our new state. Who would become our new friends? Which church would we go to? Was there really that big of a difference between barbecue and grilling out? Who would be our emergency contacts?

The distance wasn't our only major shift. We also spent our first holiday season away from our families. Away from big, festive parties and carefully planned feasts. Mom's beautifully handmade decor, the potluck of what we called "magazine food" intermixed with old family favorites, a panoply of pies, and all the other perfectly orchestrated details were noticeably absent that first year. When we moved to Tennessee, we arrived with little more than two months until Christmas morning.

Whether it's the simplicity of a banana bread or something more elaborate like baked mac and cheese, nothing says "welcome home" quite like homemade food.

A few days into unpacking the Mount Everest of color-coded boxes, our doorbell rang. To our surprise, our backdoor neighbors had come to welcome us with hugs and pumpkin bread. It was so unexpected and heartwarming, and having a little bit of homemade magic made being so far away from home easier. While living in Southern California, we moved every couple of years, and I hadn't experienced this kind of neighborliness. Something about the thoughtfulness and care made me feel like Aunt Bee had welcomed us to a modern-day Mayberry. Until this warm welcome, I'd assumed such traditions had faded with bygone eras.

Whether it's the simplicity of a banana bread or something more elaborate like baked mac and cheese, nothing says "welcome home" quite like homemade food. Especially when the cookware has yet to be unpacked and drive-thru restaurants have lost their greasy luster.

Maybe we don't see this custom as often because life has become too busy. It's easy to find ourselves deep in our own routines, and we don't often look very far outside our personal bubbles. I'd only seen this kind of neighborly behavior on black-and-white television reruns and heard about it from my grandmother's stories, but I wanted to change that for myself and for others. After receiving their homemade gift and feeling full of gratefulness for their kind gesture, I immediately vowed to do the same for any new neighbors who moved in so they too could receive the same welcome we had.

I began fulfilling this fledgling mission of feeding neighbors whenever new ones moved in. When they needed help because of a sickness, an emergency, a death in the family, or because they were working late but wanted their kids to have a wholesome dinner, I'd be there for them. Pasta dishes, soups, and stews were easiest, and then at some point I started baking bread to accompany their meals.

"You made this?" they'd ask in disbelief. "I haven't had bread like this since before we moved."

Then they shared stories of their mothers and grandmothers—or perhaps the bakery they'd reluctantly left behind—and how much my bread reminded them of home. Something so humble as the combination of flour, salt, yeast, and water was able to create a sense of nostalgia that satisfied a part of them that memories and phone calls couldn't.

Something so humble as the combination of flour, salt, yeast, and water was able to create a sense of nostalgia that satisfied a part of them that memories and phone calls couldn't.

In a town where everyone is from somewhere else, it became clear that the people on my street were not the only ones who felt a longing for home. The more I baked, the more it seemed like I could make our town feel like home, if only for a little while. Sometimes that fleeting delicious moment is enough.

Fresh Pumpkin Bread

The difference between canned pumpkin and fresh pumpkin is night and day. Fresh pumpkin has a mellow flavor that shines. Similar to a carrot cake, in this recipe the pumpkin is grated and added raw instead of as a puree. Pepitas are included for a bit of a crunch. If you want to add pecans or walnuts instead, you can substitute with whatever suits your fancy.

INGREDIENTS

2 cups all-purpose flour

1 tablespoon ground cinnamon

1 teaspoon ground nutmeg

1 teaspoon baking soda

1/4 teaspoon baking powder

1 teaspoon kosher salt

3/4 cup canola oil

1 cup white sugar

1/2 cup dark brown sugar

3 large eggs

3 cups fresh grated pumpkin

2 teaspoons vanilla extract

1 cup pepitas

DIRECTIONS

1. Preheat oven to 325 degrees.

2. In a large bowl whisk together flour, cinnamon, nutmeg, baking soda, baking powder, and salt.

3. In the bowl of an electric mixer fitted with the paddle attachment, cream together canola oil, white sugar, and brown sugar. Beat in eggs, one at a time, until light and fluffy.

4. Add the pumpkin and vanilla, and combine. Add flour mixture and combine just until it comes together. Add 3/4 cup of pepitas and fold in.

5. Pour batter into a greased loaf pan, and sprinkle remaining pepitas on top.

6. Bake for 1 hour, or until a toothpick inserted in the middle comes out clean. Cool loaf for 15 minutes. Turn out onto a cooling rack to cool completely.

Yield: one 9 x 5 x 3-inch loaf

Prep time: 15 minutes

Bake time: approximately 1 hour

Sweet Skillet Cornbread

The South may like their tea sweet, but don't you dare sweeten your cornbread. The North likes their cornbread sweet, but it's a crime to sweeten your tea. Personally, I love sweet tea *and* sweet cornbread, so this recipe is made on the sweet side. I also used three different fats in this recipe. Adding both butter and lard creates a deeper complexity of flavor while the canola oil assures that the cornbread remains moist. Because there is so little flour in this, you can easily substitute a cup of your favorite gluten-free all-purpose flour mix to suit your dietary needs.

INGREDIENTS

1 cup all-purpose flour

3/4 cup cornmeal

1 teaspoon kosher salt

1/2 teaspoon baking soda

1 teaspoon baking powder

5 tablespoons butter, divided

1/4 cup lard

1/4 cup canola or vegetable oil

3/4 cup white sugar

1 teaspoon vanilla extract

1/4 cup dark honey

2 large eggs

1 1/4 cups buttermilk

Yield: 10-inch cast iron skillet or 9-inch square pan

Prep time: 5 minutes

Bake time: 28 to 30 minutes

DIRECTIONS

1. Preheat oven to 375 degrees. Place a well-seasoned 10-inch cast-iron skillet in the oven while it's preheating.

2. In a small bowl combine flour, cornmeal, salt, baking soda, and baking powder.

3. In a small saucepan melt 4 tablespoons butter and lard, then pour into a large bowl. Add oil, sugar, vanilla, and honey. Stir to combine. Add eggs and buttermilk. Mix well. Stir flour mixture into the butter and oil mixture, but do not over mix. It's okay if it's a little lumpy.

4. Carefully remove skillet from oven, and make sure the door is closed to retain the heat. Use remaining 1 tablespoon butter to coat the hot skillet and use a pastry brush to spread.

5. Pour batter into the skillet, and carefully return to the hot oven. Bake 28 to 30 minutes or until a toothpick comes out clean.

6. Let cornbread cool for 5 to 10 minutes before serving. Serve with butter and honey.

Zucchini Walnut Bread

Perfectly dense and moist, this zucchini bread is nothing short of perfection with just the right blend of spices. Even with draining some of the water off the zucchini, the crumb still maintains a beautiful texture and amazing flavor. Add walnuts for a bit of crunch or omit them if nuts aren't your thing. It'll be delicious either way.

INGREDIENTS

4 cups grated zucchini

2 teaspoons kosher salt, divided

3 1/4 cups all-purpose flour

1 1/2 teaspoons ground cinnamon

1/2 teaspoon ground nutmeg

1 teaspoon baking soda

1/2 teaspoon baking powder

1 cup canola oil

2 cups white sugar

3 large eggs

2 teaspoons vanilla extract

1 cup chopped walnuts, divided (optional)

Yield: two 8x4 loaves

Prep time: 10 minutes

Inactive: 1 hour

Bake time: 40 to 50 minutes

DIRECTIONS

1. Preheat oven to 375 degrees.

2. Sprinkle grated zucchini with 1/2 teaspoon salt, and place in a strainer. Put the strainer in a large bowl to catch water. Allow to sit for 1 hour. Pour zucchini into a thin dish towel or a few layers of cheesecloth, and squeeze out excess water.

3. In a large bowl whisk together flour, cinnamon, nutmeg, baking soda, baking powder, and remaining 1 1/2 teaspoons salt.

4. In the bowl of an electric mixer fitted with the paddle attachment, cream together canola oil and sugar. Beat in eggs, one at a time, until light and fluffy.

5. Add shredded zucchini and vanilla and combine. Add flour mixture and combine just until it comes together. Fold in 3/4 cup of walnuts. Pour batter into two greased loaf pans, and sprinkle remaining walnuts on top.

6. Bake for 40 to 50 minutes or until a toothpick inserted in the middle comes out clean. Cool loaves for 15 minutes. Turn out onto a cooling rack to cool completely.

Coffee Crumble Loaf

Coffee cake made shareable. Welcome a new neighbor with a loaf, slice and take to a gathering, or serve as a light breakfast or dessert. Dark brown sugar and Greek yogurt add an amazing tastiness and depth of flavor.

COFFEE CRUMBLE LOAF INGREDIENTS

2 cups all-purpose flour

1 teaspoon baking soda

1/2 teaspoon baking powder

1/2 teaspoon kosher salt

3/4 cup (1 1/2 sticks) butter, softened

1 1/3 cups white sugar

3 large eggs

2 teaspoons vanilla extract

1 cup Greek yogurt or sour cream

CINNAMON CRUMBLE INGREDIENTS

1 cup dark brown sugar

1/2 cup all-purpose flour

1/4 cup (1/2 stick) butter, melted

1 teaspoon ground cinnamon

DIRECTIONS

1. Preheat oven to 375 degrees with rack placed in the center position.

2. Make the cinnamon crumble by mixing together the brown sugar, flour, melted butter, and cinnamon in a small bowl until a crumbly consistency is reached.

3. In another bowl combine flour, baking soda, baking powder, and salt and mix with a whisk.

4. In the bowl of an electric mixer fitted with the paddle attachment, cream together butter and sugar first on low to combine, and then on high for 5 minutes or until light and fluffy (almost completely white). Scrape down sides.

5. Add eggs one at a time, beating together after each addition and scraping sides of the bowl to make sure mixture is fully combined. Add vanilla and Greek yogurt, and mix on low until combined. Scrape bowl again to ensure complete mixing.

6. Add flour mixture and combine just until you don't see any more flour. Remove bowl from electric mixer, and using scraper, fold a few times, checking for even mixing. There's a fine line between overmixing and even incorporation, so don't overmix, but ensure that the texture is uniform throughout.

RECIPE CONTINUES

Yield: two 8 x 4-inch loaves or one angel food cake pan

Prep time: 10 minutes

Bake time: 35 to 40 minutes

7. Grease loaf pans, then to each pan add a quarter of the coffee cake batter, spreading evenly. Sprinkle half the cinnamon crumble over the batter. Add the remaining batter on top, spread evenly, and sprinkle generously with remaining cinnamon crumble.

8. Bake for 35 to 40 minutes until toothpick inserted in the middle comes out clean. Allow to cool for 30 minutes, turn out of pans, and allow to cool completely on a cooling rack.

Yeast Breads

Unlike quick breads, yeast breads are so called because they use yeast as a leavener, which causes carbon dioxide to form through the fermentation of sugars. This process causes the bread to rise and makes it light and airy. The dough can then be formed into various shapes and sizes. Working with yeast breads does take a little practice, but it's so worth it.

Imperfect Perfection

The art of making bread is just that: art. It's a lifelong journey of perfecting technique, subtly tweaking things along the way, and finding yourself making different breads over time as your taste and ability develops. It's trying something new and being willing to eat whatever comes out of the oven in hopes of learning from your mistakes.

When I first began learning how to bake bread, I didn't know what I was doing. I would follow a recipe and what would come out of the oven didn't look like the picture printed next to the text. It was flat, deflated, pale, and looked like someone had hurt its feelings. I wondered what I had done wrong and why it wasn't instantly perfect that first time. Bread is not as predictable as cake out of a box.

Maybe I'm just bad at this, I thought as I took another bite of a hot slice slathered in butter. I was still unaware of one of the cardinal rules of bread. Well, I suppose two, really. First, never cut into bread just out of the oven. The starches need to set and cutting too early will make the crumb appear underbaked. Second, if I can't wait for bread to cool before eating it, I need to make two loaves so I can satisfy my craving for hot-out-of-the-oven bread and still end up with a proper loaf for later. Sometimes you have to live your best life. In all sincerity, that's one reason why many of the recipes in this book make more than one loaf. One for you now, and one for sharing later.

In the following years after I baked that first sad loaf, I learned about the personality of my ingredients. Even with a simple loaf containing only flour, salt, yeast, and water, it is possible to change a hundred different things and create a hundred different loaves. Different water-to-flour ratio means different-size holes in the crumb. Different baking temperatures mean different kinds of crust. Different rise times mean different flavors. Different oven humidity means a change in oven spring. Different flour combinations mean a multitude of options. As you learn to bake bread, you'll discover—just as I had to—one of the only things that needs to remain constant is your willingness to mess up without getting discouraged. After all, it is just flour.

Even with a simple loaf containing only flour, salt, yeast, and water, it is possible to change a hundred different things and create a hundred different loaves.

Some of the breads I've created came out better than I've ever made. Others could have been used as a doorstop. Some boasted excellent flavor but were woefully ugly, while others looked picture-perfect but lacked flavor. Each attempt was an education in what I had done wrong the time before and offered clues on how to proceed the next time. There just needed to be a next time in order to improve. Thank goodness I'm stubborn.

As I tell my baking students, you're never done learning with bread.

One of my favorite things about my Rustic Artisan Bread recipe is that you can tweak it ever so slightly and create a different flavor. Allowing it to cold ferment overnight in the fridge after mixing the ingredients and an initial two-hour rise gives it a stronger, more intense flavor. Form it cold and allow it to rise as it comes to room temperature. Folding the dough rather than punching it rejuvenates the gluten, allowing for longer rise times and deeper complexity of flavor.

Adding a bit more flour so the dough is not as slack offers a different texture. So will baking at a cooler temperature for a longer period of time. Replacing a small percentage of the flour with an equal amount of whole wheat, spelt, or another type of flour makes a different loaf completely. Adding a tablespoon or two of olive oil turns this dough into an excellent thin crust for pizza.

Before embarking on the creative adventure of developing your own concoctions from the basic recipe, make it as-is first. Learn the dough's personality and how it reacts in different weather and levels of humidity. Discover how the warmth of a room will determine how quickly it rises. Accept that bread will move at its own pace and find ways to push it in the direction you want it to go. Learn how to create perfect slash marks on your bread. It's like learning how to use a knife as a paintbrush, and both take practice.

As I tell my baking students, you're never done learning with bread. You're never done discovering what it can become. It's a living organism, so it's not just something you make; it's something you nurture and cultivate. It's an adventure with multiple destinations. If you are a novice, as we all once were, do not become discouraged if your first, second, or even tenth loaf doesn't come out perfectly. Just do as we've all done: slather it with butter and try again. After all, it's just flour, salt, yeast, and water.

Rustic Artisan Bread

This four-ingredient bread was my personal springboard into the world of artisan bread. Simple in assembly, this bread is about the time it takes to develop flavor, as well as folding and forming techniques. Since this bread is considered lean—meaning it has no fat—whatever is spread on top of this bread will have a far more intense flavor. Use the bread as toast, to make a sandwich, or even as a crostini or for French toast.

INGREDIENTS

3 tablespoons active dry yeast

4 cups warm water

8 cups all-purpose flour

3 tablespoons kosher salt

cornmeal

Yield: 3 loaves

Prep time: 6 to 24 hours

Bake time: 30 to 40 minutes

DIRECTIONS

1. In a large bowl proof yeast by adding warm water (no hotter than 115 degrees) to yeast and mix together with a whisk. Allow to sit undisturbed for approximately 10 minutes. You're looking for foam to form on the water.

2. While yeast is proofing, combine flour and salt in a large bowl. Once yeast has become foamy, add the flour mixture to the yeast. With the handle of a wooden spoon or dough whisk, stir to combine all ingredients. Dough will still be a little shaggy. Do not overmix. Scrape the sides of the bowl clean. Cover with plastic wrap (not touching dough), and allow to hydrate for at least 2 hours, but as long as 12 hours. The longer you let the dough ferment, the more developed the flavor will become.

3. If you would like to cold ferment, at this point the dough can be refrigerated for up to two weeks in an airtight container. When you are ready to bake, pull off a pound of dough and form into the desired loaf shape, coat the bottom with cornmeal, place on the baking sheet, and allow to rise as the dough comes to room temperature. Bake as directed below.

RECIPE CONTINUES

4. Turn out dough onto floured surface. Begin by folding dough to the middle in the following pattern: top, bottom, left, and right. Dough will begin to firm. Stop when dough will not fold without tearing. Place the dough, fold side down, back into the bowl, and allow to rise for 1 more hour.

5. Separate dough into three equal parts and form into balls. Set on floured surface for 15 minutes. Form each loaf into baguette, boule, or oval shape. Press formed loaf, seam side down, into cornmeal to coat the bottom, and place on baking sheet. Cover with a flour sack cloth and allow to rise until not quite doubled in size.

6. Adjust shelf in oven to the middle rack. Preheat oven to 450 degrees halfway through rise time to ensure oven is very hot. Ten minutes prior to baking, place an oven-proof dish containing 1 to 2 inches of water in the oven to create a steam bath.

7. When loaves are ready, slash top of bread using a razor (lâme) or a very sharp knife. You can get creative with your slashing, but make sure there are at least a few to allow steam to escape.

8. Bake bread for 30 to 40 minutes; longer if you like a nice deep brown, thick crust. Some light charring is okay and will add flavor.

9. Remove carefully from oven, and place on a cooling rack to cool. You can also prop up loaves on the edge of a cutting board or sheet pan as long as the bottoms are not making full contact with any surface to prevent steam from making them soggy.

10. Cool loaves completely before cutting to allow starches to become stable.

Roasted Garlic Artisan Bread

Taking the Rustic Artisan Bread to the next level, roasted garlic and fresh rosemary are added to the dough, making this the perfect addition to everything from Italian dishes to steak and potatoes. This bread also works beautifully in the Asparagus, Pancetta, and Gouda Strata found on page 115.

INGREDIENTS

4 teaspoons active dry yeast

2 cups warm water

4 cups all-purpose flour

4 teaspoons kosher salt

2 tablespoons roasted garlic, mashed

2 tablespoons fresh rosemary, chopped

cornmeal

Yield: 1 loaf

Prep time: 6 to 24 hours

Bake time: 30 to 40 minutes

DIRECTIONS

1. In a large bowl proof yeast by adding warm water (no hotter than 115 degrees) to yeast and mix together with a whisk. Allow to sit undisturbed for approximately 10 minutes. You're looking for foam to form on the water.

2. Combine flour and salt in another large bowl. Once yeast has become foamy, add the flour mixture to the yeast. With the handle of a wooden spoon or dough whisk, stir to combine all ingredients. Dough will still be a little shaggy. Do not overmix. Scrape the sides of the bowl clean. Cover with plastic wrap (not touching dough), and allow to hydrate for at least 2 hours, but as long as 12 hours. The longer you let the dough ferment, the more developed the flavor will become.

3. If you would like to cold ferment, at this point the dough can be refrigerated for up to two weeks in an airtight container. Form into the desired loaf shape, coat the bottom with cornmeal, place on the baking sheet, and allow to rise as the dough comes to room temperature. Bake as directed below.

RECIPE CONTINUES

4. While the dough is rising, roast the garlic. See directions below.

5. Turn out dough onto floured surface. Begin by folding dough to the middle in the following pattern: top, bottom, left, and right. Dough will begin to firm. Stop when dough will not fold without tearing. Place the dough, fold side down, back into the bowl, and allow to rise for 1 more hour.

6. Lay dough flat, spreading and sprinkling the desired amounts of garlic and rosemary over the bread. Fold bread four times to incorporate the ingredients. Form the loaf into boule shapes. Press formed loaf, seam side down, into cornmeal to coat the bottom, and place on baking sheet with 4 to 5 inches between to avoid touching. Cover with a flour sack cloth and allow to rise until not quite doubled in size.

7. Adjust shelf in oven to the middle rack. Preheat oven to 450 degrees halfway through rise time to ensure oven is very hot. Ten minutes prior to baking, place an oven-proof dish containing 1 to 2 inches of water in the oven to create a steam bath.

8. When loaves are ready, slash top of bread using a razor (lâme) or a very sharp knife to create slashing. You can get creative with your slashing, but make sure there are at least a few to allow steam to escape.

9. Bake bread for 30 to 40 minutes. Longer if you like a nice deep brown, thick crust. Some light charring is okay and will add flavor.

10. Remove carefully from oven, and place on a cooling rack to cool. You can also prop up on the edge of a cutting board or sheet pan as long as the bottoms are not making full contact with any surface to prevent steam from making them soggy.

11. Cool loaves completely before cutting to allow starches to become stable.

Roasted Garlic

INGREDIENTS

1 large head garlic

olive oil

kosher salt

fresh cracked black pepper

DIRECTIONS FOR ROASTED GARLIC

1. Cut off the top of the head of garlic. Place on a piece of foil. Drizzle with olive oil, and sprinkle with salt and pepper. Seal the garlic bulb in the foil.

2. Roast in the oven at 400 degrees for 40 minutes, or until the garlic cloves are very soft. Remove the garlic from the oven and allow to cool.

3. Remove the cloves from the head of garlic and mash. Use the amount needed in this recipe and blend the rest with butter for use as a spread.

White Bread

When I think of the quintessential white bread, this is exactly what comes to mind. Perfect for your favorite combo of peanut butter and jelly, an awesome grilled cheese, or turkey and Swiss. You can't go wrong with this classic loaf. Make multiple loaves at once to save on time. It freezes well too!

INGREDIENTS

1 1/2 tablespoons active dry yeast

1 1/2 cups warm water

1 1/2 cups whole milk, scalded and cooled

1/4 cup white sugar

2 teaspoons kosher salt

3 tablespoons butter, melted

7 cups all-purpose flour

Yield: 2 large or 3 medium loaves

Prep time: 20 minutes

Bake time: small loaves 25 to 30 minutes, large loaves 40 to 45 minutes

Total time: 4 to 5 hours

DIRECTIONS

1. In the bowl of an electric mixer fitted with the dough hook attachment, proof yeast in warm water (no hotter than 115 degrees) for 5 minutes, or until surface starts to foam. Add the scalded and cooled milk, sugar, salt, and melted butter, and stir together.

2. Add 4 cups of flour and combine until even consistently. Then add the rest of the flour, 1 cup at a time, until the dough pulls away from the sides of the bowl. The last cup should be added just a sprinkle at a time so not too much flour is added (it's okay if you don't use all 7 cups).

3. Turn out the dough onto a floured surface, sprinkle the top of the dough with flour, and knead it approximately 20 times, or until dough is smooth. If dough is still sticky, sprinkle lightly with flour.

4. Place dough into a greased bowl, cover with plastic wrap, and allow to rise for 1 to 1 1/2 hours, or until dough is doubled in size.

5. Turn out dough onto a clean surface, cut into 2 or 3 loaves, and form into balls. Allow dough to rest for 20 minutes.

RECIPE CONTINUES

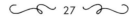

6. To form dough into loaves, pat into a flat rectangle the same length as the pan and approximately four times the width. Use a rolling pan if needed and roll into a log. Grease loaf pans and place dough into pans. Large pans should be 9 x 5 inches and medium loaves should be 8 ½ x 4 inches.

7. Brush loaves with melted butter, cover with plastic wrap, and allow to double in size so that loaves are 2 inches taller than the pan, approximately 1 hour.

8. Bake loaves at 400 degrees. Smaller loaves will bake for 25 to 30 minutes. Larger loaves will bake 40 to 45 minutes. The loaves will sound hollow when tapped. Turn loaves out onto a cooling rack immediately. Allow to cool completely before cutting and/or packaging.

Sustenance

If you lined up all the Allen girls and a few of us grandkids, you would notice one incredibly distinct feature: we all have Great-Gramma Viola's great big, brown eyes. Her picture hung on the wall among a collage of family photos in my parents' home. Thick, black, wavy curls were neatly combed into a classic 1940s style. Her cheerful cotton floral dress draped over her thin frame. The expression on her face was neither smiling nor frowning, but rather one of quiet determination. Although she was still young, her eyes gave away the hardships she had endured.

Great-Gramma was born to a poor family in Missouri. She married young and soon found herself raising her four children . . . alone. She worked as a servant, baking bread on the side, trying hard to sustain her family. She kept her sourdough starter in a jar, feeding it each day so it would continue to feed them.

Then the Great Depression hit and her source of income was gone. Her home life grew unbearable and she knew she needed to escape to save them. Her older children helped her pack up the car, and the five of them left "Misery" and headed for California. Her eldest son, James, took the wheel and she clung tightly to her jar of starter for the entire trip. That precious jar filled with flour and wild yeast was her family's lifeline. She protected it as if it was gold. It was like a scene out of *The Grapes of Wrath*.

Once they reached the safety of the West Coast, far away from the troubles of home, Great-Gramma began to bake again. Even as arthritis began to affect her joints and she could no longer stand for very long, she was still able to bake every day and feed her family with her bread. She had sustained her children during the hardest of times with her gift.

Through every snowstorm, and even during the pandemic, it was common to go to the grocery store and find empty shelves where an aisle of bread should be. It's somewhat comical, especially in the South where it doesn't snow much at all and yet everyone panic-purchases every available loaf. In other areas, and in other circumstances, bread becomes such an important part of survival.

In the Lord's Prayer, there's a line asking for daily bread, regular sustenance with which to survive. As much as we need food, we need love and caring too. Great-Gramma Viola gave so much of herself to raise her children and took in others who didn't have parents. She never made much money, but her gifts and her heart for serving others made her rich.

At the bakery, we talk a lot about feeding people. Baking bread, breaking bread, and bringing a community together. We adopted the quote "Give us this day" as a daily reminder to our staff and to the community that we were there to sustain others. Not just with baked goods, but with words of encouragement and sometimes prayer. Feeding our customers with kindness and love is just as important, just as "daily bread" means so much more than actual bread. We are there to fill not just bellies, but hearts and souls too. Viola's legacy lives on.

Honey Oat Wheat Bread

The longer you let the dough ferment, the richer the flavor will be. In this recipe, we begin with a sponge that ferments overnight. The bran in the whole wheat will soften as it ferments, bringing to life an incredibly complex, slightly sweet, and wonderful flavor. This bread is perfect for sandwiches and toast.

SPONGE INGREDIENTS

$3/4$ cup warm water

$3/4$ cup whole wheat flour

$1/4$ cup rolled oats

$1/4$ teaspoon active dry yeast

DOUGH INGREDIENTS

$3/4$ cup warm water

1 teaspoon active dry yeast

$1\frac{1}{2}$ cups bread flour

$3/4$ cup whole wheat flour

$1/3$ cup wildflower or clover honey

$2\frac{1}{2}$ teaspoons kosher salt

$1/4$ cup rolled oats

$1/4$ cup cornmeal

DIRECTIONS

1. To make the sponge, in a bowl mix together warm water (no hotter than 115 degrees), whole wheat flour, oats, and yeast. Cover and allow to ferment overnight, 8 to 12 hours. The longer the ferment, the more complex the flavor.

2. For the dough, in a measuring cup whisk together water (no hotter than 115 degrees) and yeast, and allow to proof for 10 minutes. You're looking for foam to form on the water.

3. Meanwhile, add bread flour, whole wheat flour, honey, salt, oats, and the sponge to the bowl of an electric mixer fitted with the dough hook attachment. Once yeast has become foamy, add it to the flour mixture. Mix the ingredients together on the lowest speed until the dough comes together and pulls away from the sides of the bowl. If the dough is still sticky, you can add more bread flour, 1 tablespoon at a time until it clears. Allow the dough to sit for 15 minutes, undisturbed, to hydrate. Mix again for 1 minute on medium speed until it again clears the sides of the bowl. Move dough to a clean bowl coated with nonstick spray, cover with a tea towel, and allow to rise for 1 hour, or until doubled in size.

RECIPE CONTINUES

Yield: 1 loaf

Inactive time: 12 hours

Active time: 40 minutes

Prep time: 20 minutes

Bake time: 25 to 30 minutes

4. Turn out dough onto a lightly floured surface. Form loaf into an oval or batard (football shape). Seam side down, press the loaf into cornmeal to coat the bottom, then transfer to a sheet pan. Cover with a tea towel and allow to rise until almost double in size.

5. Place an oven-proof dish containing 1 to 2 inches of water in the oven to create a steam bath. Then preheat oven to 425 degrees.

6. Using a very sharp paring knife or a lâme, slash bread to allow steam to escape. Spritz loaf with water, and sprinkle loaf with more oats if desired.

7. Bake for 20 to 25 minutes, or until loaf has browned and sounds hollow when tapped on the bottom. If it's not brown or hollow sounding, bake in additional 5-minute increments until it is. Once baked, move loaf to a cooling rack and allow to cool completely.

Focaccia

A staple in Italian cuisine, focaccia is a delightfully rustic flatbread baked in olive oil. This recipe creates a lofty loaf that's perfect for sandwiches or great for accompanying a variety of meals. It can also be baked in smaller sizes to be served individually, or in a more rustic shape, for breaking and sharing.

DOUGH INGREDIENTS

5 cups all-purpose flour

2 cups warm water

1 tablespoon kosher salt

1 tablespoon active dry yeast

1/2 cup olive oil

TOPPINGS

fresh rosemary

fresh thyme

fresh oregano

1/2 cup olive oil

coarse sea salt

fresh cracked black pepper

red pepper flakes (optional)

DIRECTIONS

1. In the bowl of an electric mixer fitted with the dough hook attachment, combine flour, warm water (no hotter than 115 degrees), salt, yeast, and olive oil on low until ingredients are incorporated. Turn up to second speed setting, and mix until dough comes together, adding extra flour as necessary for dough to pull away from the sides of the bowl. Turn off machine, allowing dough to rest and hydrate for 10 minutes. Turn on second speed again, and knead just until dough is soft and smooth, approximately 2 minutes.

2. Transfer dough to a bowl coated in nonstick spray, turning dough under to create a smooth surface. Cover with plastic wrap or tea towel, and allow to rise until doubled in size, approximately 1 hour.

3. Roughly chop rosemary, thyme, and oregano.

4. Coat sheet pan with 1/2 cup olive oil, making sure the entire bottom is completely covered.

RECIPE CONTINUES

Yield: 1 sheet pan

Prep time: 30 minutes

Inactive time: 2 hours

Bake time: 25 to 30 minutes

5. Without punching down, carefully move risen dough to sheet pan and gently press dough to fit pan. Flip once halfway through, and poke deep holes into the dough as you spread it to all corners and sides of the pan. If dough becomes resistant to spreading, allow to rest for a few minutes before continuing. Tugging at the corners of the dough to help get to the right size may be necessary.

6. Sprinkle dough with coarse sea salt, pepper, and herbs. Allow the dough to rise until it has completely filled the pan and begins to rise above the sides of the pan.

7. Place an oven-proof dish containing 1 to 2 inches of water on the bottom rack of the oven to create a steam bath. Halfway through the final rise, preheat oven to 375 degrees.

8. When dough is ready, bake for 25 to 30 minutes, or until crust is golden brown.

Cinnamon Braided Brioche

As the ultimate French toast bread, brioche is already pure bliss. Braid in a decadent cinnamon filling, and it becomes absolutely legendary. Whether you decide to attempt the two-stranded Zopf (pictured) or stick with a classic three-stranded braid, the most important thing to remember is to make sure you get a good seal on each rope so the cinnamon filling doesn't leak out!

INGREDIENTS

3 3/4 cups bread flour

1 cup all-purpose flour

1 teaspoon kosher salt

1 tablespoon active dry yeast

1/4 cup white sugar

3/4 cup (1 1/2 sticks) butter, cubed and softened

2 large eggs

1/2 cup whole milk

1 cup warm water

Cinnamon Filling (page 169)

1 large egg

2 tablespoons water

Yield: 2 loaves

Prep time: 1 hour

Inactive time: 2 hours

Bake time: 25 to 30 minutes

DIRECTIONS

1. In the bowl of an electric mixer fitted with the dough hook attachment, mix together bread flour, all-purpose flour, salt, yeast, and sugar.

2. Add softened butter cubes to flour mixture and mix for 2 to 3 minutes.

3. Add 2 eggs, milk, and water (no hotter than 115 degrees) to flour, and combine until dough comes together and pulls away from the sides of the bowl. Dough should be soft and stretchy. Turn off mixer and allow dough to sit for 10 minutes to rest and hydrate. Start mixer again for 1 minute until dough pulls away from the sides of the bowl again.

4. Move dough to a clean bowl coated in nonstick spray, cover with plastic wrap, and allow to rise for 1 hour or until doubled in size.

5. Make cinnamon filling on page 169.

RECIPE CONTINUES

6. Turn out dough onto a floured surface. Cut into four to six even pieces (four if you want two strands, six if you want three strands). Form pieces into small ovals and allow to rest for 5 minutes. Starting with one loaf at a time, roll each piece into a 12 to 14-inch rope. Then flatten each piece with your hand, and roll flat with a rolling pin, creating very long ovals. Spread cinnamon filling over the dough, leaving a long strip bare at the top of the dough. It will be impossible to seal the ropes if there is filling on the ends. Roll each piece into a long, thin rope, and seal the edges and ends. Repeat process with each braid.

7. Place finished braids onto a baking sheet lined with parchment. Cover with a tea towel or plastic wrap, and allow to double in size, approximately 1 hour.

8. Place an oven-proof dish containing 1 to 2 inches of water on the bottom rack of the oven to create a steam bath. Then preheat oven to 425 degrees.

9. Whisk together two tablespoons of water and egg to create egg wash. Be sure to thoroughly break up the egg whites.

10. When the loaves have doubled, using a pastry brush, coat each loaf thoroughly with egg wash.

11. Bake for 25 to 30 minutes, or until crusts are a dark brown.

12. Move loaves to a cooling rack to cool completely before cutting.

Chocolate Hazelnut Babka

Made on buttery brioche, this decadent loaf of babka is what chocolatey dreams are made of. This recipe makes two loaves, but it's best to make each loaf separately to maintain consistency in shape and size. Additionally, I find using the back of a spoon is the best tool for achieving the most even coverage of the hazelnut spread.

INGREDIENTS

3 ¾ cups bread flour

1 cup all-purpose flour

1 tablespoon kosher salt

1 tablespoon active dry yeast

¼ cup white sugar

¾ cup (1 ½ sticks) butter, cubed and softened

2 large eggs

½ cup whole milk

1 cup warm water

1 cup hazelnut spread, divided

½ cup chopped hazelnuts, divided

Yield: 2 loaves

Prep time: 25 minutes

Inactive time: 2 hours

Bake time: 25 minutes

DIRECTIONS

1. In the bowl of an electric mixer fitted with the dough hook attachment, mix together bread flour, all-purpose flour, salt, yeast, and sugar.

2. Add softened butter cubes to flour mixture and mix for 2 to 3 minutes.

3. Add eggs, milk, and water to flour, and combine until dough comes together and pulls away from the sides of the bowl. Dough should be soft and stretchy. Turn off mixer and allow dough to sit for 10 minutes to rest and hydrate. Start mixer again for 1 minute until dough pulls away from the sides of the bowl again.

4. Move dough to a clean bowl coated in nonstick spray, cover with plastic wrap, and allow to rise for 1 hour or until doubled in size.

RECIPE CONTINUES

5. Turn out dough onto a floured surface and separate into two equal parts. Allow to rest for 10 minutes. For each loaf, sprinkle the top of the dough with more flour. Form dough into a rectangular shape. Using a rolling pin, roll dough into a rectangle approximately $1/4$ inch thick. Smear hazelnut spread over dough, leaving an inch at the top clean so it will seal. Sprinkle half of the chopped hazelnuts evenly over the spread. Begin rolling the bottom edge of the dough toward the top, forming a log, and seal. Roll the seam to the bottom, allowing the weight of the log to hold everything in place.

6. Using a sharp knife, cut the log in half lengthwise so you have two long strands. Allow the halves to fall open, exposing the pattern of the hazelnut spread. Twist the two strands together, making sure the cut edges face up so the hazelnut spread is visible. Seal ends and transfer twist to a greased loaf pan and cover with plastic wrap. Allow loaf to rise until it's approximately an inch taller than the pan.

7. Place an oven-proof dish containing 1 to 2 inches of water in the oven to create a steam bath. Approximately 10 minutes before loaf is ready to bake, preheat oven to 375 degrees with rack placed in the center position.

8. Bake for 20 to 25 minutes, or until crust is dark brown and shiny. If crust browns too quickly, cover with foil.

9. Allow to cool in the pan for 20 minutes before turning out to cool completely on a rack before eating.

10. Store leftover babka at room temperature for up to 3 days. To store longer, wrap well and freeze. Refrigeration will dry out the bread quickly.

Jalapeño Cheddar Bread

Brioche is typically a sweeter bread, but when you remove some of the sugar and add cheddar and jalapeños, the brioche is elevated to a whole new level. Lacing the soft, buttery loaves with the spice and cheese creates an amazing bread that makes the perfect sandwich bread. You can adjust the heat level by leaving out some of the jalapeño or adding up to a tablespoon of finely diced Serrano chilis.

INGREDIENTS

4 jalapeños

3 3/4 cups bread flour

1 cup all-purpose flour

1 tablespoon kosher salt

1 tablespoon active dry yeast

2 tablespoons white sugar

3/4 cup (1 1/2 sticks) butter, cubed and softened

1 1/2 cups sharp cheddar, divided

2 large eggs

1/2 cup whole milk

1 cup warm water

Yield: 2 loaves

Prep time: 25 minutes

Inactive time: 2 hours

Bake time: 25 minutes

DIRECTIONS

1. Slice two of the jalapeños into rounds and set aside. Dice the other two jalapeños. If you like the bread spicy, you can leave in the seeds. If you prefer milder bread, remove the seeds from the peppers.

2. In the bowl of an electric mixer fitted with the dough hook attachment, mix together bread flour, all-purpose flour, salt, yeast, and sugar. Add softened butter cubes to flour mixture and mix for 2 to 3 minutes. Add the diced jalapeños and 1 cup of cheddar and combine.

3. Add eggs, milk, and water (no hotter than 115 degrees) to flour and combine until dough comes together and pulls away from the sides of the bowl. Dough should be soft and stretchy. Turn off mixer and allow dough to sit for 10 minutes to rest and hydrate. Start mixer again for 1 minute until dough pulls away from the sides of the bowl again.

4. Move dough to a clean bowl coated in nonstick spray, cover with plastic wrap, and allow to rise for 1 hour or until doubled in size.

RECIPE CONTINUES

5. Turn out dough onto a floured surface and sprinkle the top of the dough with more flour. Divide the dough in half and allow to rest for 5 minutes. Pat each of the loaves flat and roll into a log. Place each of the logs into a greased 9 x 5-inch loaf pan. Sprinkle the rest of the cheese over the loaves, and add the jalapeño rounds to the tops of the loaves. Allow loaves to rise until they're approximately 1 inch taller than the pans.

6. Place an oven-proof dish containing 1 to 2 inches of water in the oven to create a steam bath. Approximately 10 minutes before loaf is ready to bake, preheat oven to 375 degrees with rack placed in the center position.

7. When the loaves are ready, bake for 20 to 25 minutes, or until crust is dark brown and shiny.

8. Turn loaves out of pans immediately and allow to cool completely. Then slice and enjoy!

Cuban Bread

This authentic Cuban bread makes the absolutely best sub sandwiches. Using *manteca* (lard) to enrich this dough gives it a fantastic savory flavor. Whether you want to create a *Pan con Bistec*, a traditional Cuban sandwich, or even make tartines or hors d'oeuvres, this is the perfect loaf.

INGREDIENTS

2 ²/₃ cups bread flour

2 ²/₃ cups all-purpose flour

1 ²/₃ cups warm water

1 ¹/₂ tablespoons active dry yeast

1 tablespoon white sugar

1 tablespoon kosher salt

3 ounces lard, melted

Yield: 2 loaves

Prep time: 20 minutes

Inactive time: 2 hours

Bake time: 18 minutes

DIRECTIONS

1. Mix bread flour and all-purpose flour together thoroughly in a bowl.

2. In the bowl of an electric mixer fitted with the dough hook attachment, add water (no hotter than 115 degrees), yeast, and sugar. Whisk together and allow to proof for 5 minutes. Add salt after the 5 minutes.

3. With mixer on low, add 1 cup of flour mixture and a few tablespoons of the melted lard at a time. Wait until flour is completely worked in before adding more. You will end up incorporating all of the lard, but you will still have some flour left over. You want the dough to remain soft, so you'll just put in what you need. Once dough is smooth, cover bowl with plastic wrap, and allow to rise until double in size, approximately 1 hour.

4. Turn out dough onto a floured surface and divide in half. Form each ball into a baguette shape, and place on a baking sheet lined with parchment. Allow to rise uncovered until double in size, approximately 1 hour.

5. Approximately 15 minutes before loaves are fully risen, preheat oven to 425 degrees.

RECIPE CONTINUES

6. Using a very sharp knife (or lâme), slash baguettes from end to end to release steam while baking.

7. Bake for 15 to 18 minutes, or until crusts are golden brown and bottoms sound hollow when tapped. Move loaves to a cooling rack and allow to cool completely before slicing.

Buttered Knots

If happiness is hot buttered bread, then unbridled joy is a buttered knot. At the bakery, we'd call these twice-buttered knots since they're brushed both before and after they come out of the oven. In fact, if there was anything I wanted to "taste test for quality control" before we'd send them to the front, this would easily be it. The knots are crispy on the outside and soft in the middle, with so much flavor they'll perfectly complement any meal. This recipe makes a ton of them because you'd "butter knot" run out.

INGREDIENTS

5 cups all-purpose flour

2 tablespoons active dry yeast

1 tablespoon kosher salt, plus extra for sprinkling

2 tablespoons butter, softened

1 3/4 cup warm water

1/2 cup (1 stick) butter, melted

Yield: 30 rolls

Prep time: 25 minutes

Inactive time: 2 hours

Bake time: 15 to 20 minutes

DIRECTIONS

1. In the bowl of an electric mixer fitted with the dough hook attachment, combine flour, yeast, and salt. Add the softened butter and mix for 2 minutes. Add water (no hotter than 115 degrees) and mix until dough comes together and clears the sides of the bowl, adding a little more flour as necessary. Allow the dough to rest for 10 minutes in the bowl, and then knead again for 1 minute. Transfer dough to a greased bowl and allow to rise for 1 hour.

2. Turn out the dough onto a floured surface, and weigh into 3-ounce balls. Form each ball into an oval shape and set aside. Once all the dough has been weighed, roll each of the ovals into a rope and tie into a knot. Place the knots 2 inches apart on a baking sheet lined with parchment. Allow to rise for 1 hour or until doubled in size.

RECIPE CONTINUES

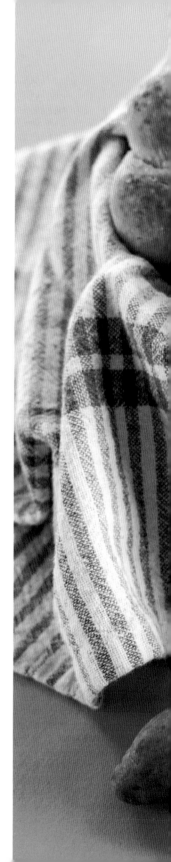

3. Ten minutes before the dough has fully risen, preheat oven to 375 degrees. Brush each knot with butter and bake for 15 to 20 minutes or until knots are golden brown. Brush again with melted butter immediately after taking them out of the oven and sprinkle them lightly with kosher salt or flaky sea salt. Serve warm.

4. To reheat, bake knots at 350 degrees for 5 minutes or until they're warm all the way through.

5. To store, keep them in a zip-top bag at room temperature for up to 3 days, or double-bagged in the freezer for up to 1 month.

Great-Aunt Ruby's Icebox Rolls

These were the first rolls I ever learned how to form with my gramma. Ever present for holiday dinners, these were baked in muffin tins as clover rolls. Don't wait for a holiday to make these, though. They're so good, I'd eat them year-round. What's great about this dough is you can keep it refrigerated for up to a week and pull from it as needed.

INGREDIENTS

2 1/2 teaspoons active dry yeast

1 teaspoon plus 1/3 cup white sugar, divided

1/2 cup warm water

1 cup warm milk

1/3 cup butter, melted

2 teaspoons kosher salt

1 large egg, beaten

5 to 5 1/2 cups all-purpose flour

Yield: 24 rolls

Prep time: 25 minutes

Inactive time: 3 hours

Bake time: 15 to 20 minutes

Time: 4 1/2 hours

DIRECTIONS

1. In the bowl of an electric mixer fitted with the dough hook attachment, dissolve yeast and 1 teaspoon of sugar in warm water (no hotter than 115 degrees). Allow to stand for 10 minutes.

2. Add milk, melted butter, remaining 1/3 cup sugar, salt, and egg, and mix on low to combine. Add flour 2 cups at a time until a dough forms and clings to the hook. Allow dough to rest for 10 minutes. Then knead for approximately 2 minutes, or until the dough becomes smooth.

3. Place dough in a clean greased bowl, turning once to grease all sides. Cover with plastic wrap and refrigerate for at least 2 hours.

4. To shape dough, separate into 1-ounce balls of dough, and roll each into a ball. Place 3 balls in each cup of a greased muffin tin. Cover with plastic wrap, and allow to rise until double in size, approximately 1 hour.

5. Preheat oven to 425 degrees when rolls are nearly double in size.

6. When rolls have risen, remove plastic wrap and bake for 15 to 20 minutes or until golden brown. Remove from oven and remove from pan immediately. Serve warm with butter.

Easy Soft Pretzels—3 Ways

While pretzels are typically made with a boiling baking soda bath, these pretzels forgo that process so they're quick and easy for the beginner baker. First, there's the original pretzel sprinkled with sea salt for the purist. Then there are a couple of variations for those who prefer a sweet or spicy option. Want to get creative? Feel free to add your own twist!

INGREDIENTS

1 tablespoon kosher salt

3 tablespoons white sugar

1 tablespoon active dry yeast

1 to 1 1/4 pounds bread flour

3 tablespoons canola oil

1 tablespoon distilled white vinegar

1 1/4 cups warm water

1 large egg

sea salt

Yield: 8 pretzels

Prep time: 30 minutes

Inactive time: 2 hours

Bake time: 15–20 minutes

Time: 3 1/2 hours

DIRECTIONS

1. Add salt, sugar, yeast, and 1 pound of flour into the bowl of an electric mixer fitted with the dough hook attachment. Stir to combine. Add oil, vinegar, and water, and mix on low until dough comes together. If dough is not pulling away from the sides of the bowl, add a little more flour at a time until it does. Stop mixer and allow 10 minutes for dough to hydrate.

2. In a small bowl whisk together egg and 2 tablespoons water, making an egg wash.

3. Using the mixer, knead dough just until it pulls away from sides of bowl. Turn out dough into a large greased bowl, and cover with plastic wrap. Allow to rise for 1 hour or until dough is double in size.

4. Turn out dough onto floured surface. Weigh out pretzels to 5 ounces each, and form into ovals. Let dough relax for 5 minutes. This will make them easier to roll.

5. Roll each dough ball into a long rope. Form dough into a circle with two long ends, double twist, and bring ends to the opposite side of the circle.

RECIPE CONTINUES

Pinch ends to attach, creating the pretzel shape. Place finished pretzels on a baking sheet lined with parchment. Allow to rise until doubled in size.

6. Preheat oven to 400 degrees approximately 10 minutes before pretzels have finished rising.

7. Brush with egg wash, and sprinkle with sea salt. Bake pretzels 15 to 20 minutes until they're golden brown.

8. Enjoy warm.

Jalapeño Pretzels: Once pretzels are formed, sprinkle with sharp cheddar and add sliced jalapeños on top. Allow to rise until doubled in size and bake as directed.

Cinnamon Sugar Pretzels: Make a mixture of cinnamon and sugar. Melt 1 stick of butter in a container large enough to fully coat the pretzels. Make the pretzels as directed above, but do not use egg wash. Instead, once the pretzels are baked and still hot, dunk each one in butter and then coat in cinnamon and sugar.

Soft Kaiser Rolls

While traditional Kaiser rolls are usually a hard bread, these offer a new spin, creating soft, fragrant rolls fit for sandwiches or even a burger bun.

INGREDIENTS

2 cups bread flour

2 cups all-purpose flour

1 1/4 cup warm water

2 teaspoons white sugar

2 teaspoons kosher salt

1 tablespoon active dry yeast

2 ounces lard, melted

1 large egg

black and white sesame seeds

Yield: 8 rolls

Prep time: 30 minutes

Inactive time: 2 hours

Bake time: 15 to 20 minutes

DIRECTIONS

1. With a whisk, mix bread flour and all-purpose flour together thoroughly in a bowl.

2. In the bowl of an electric mixer, mix together water (no hotter than 115 degrees), sugar, salt, and yeast with a whisk. Then, using the dough hook attachment, turn mixer on low and alternate adding 1/2 cup of flour and 1 tablespoon of lard, combining fully before the next addition. Continue adding until a soft, smooth dough forms, clings to the hook, and pulls away from the sides of the bowl. You will use all of the lard but likely not all of the flour.

3. Move dough to a clean bowl coated with nonstick spray, and allow to double in size, approximately 1 hour.

4. Separate dough into 8 equal parts, and form into ovals. Roll each one into a rope, being careful not to stretch outward when you roll. Pressure should be downward without stretching to avoid tearing the dough. Tie each section into a knot in the middle, then tuck the ends around again until a six-petal flour forms. Once forming is complete, place each roll 4 inches apart on a sheet pan lined with parchment paper. Allow to rise for 1 hour or until doubled in size.

RECIPE CONTINUES

5. Place an oven-proof dish containing 1 to 2 inches of water in the oven to create a steam bath. Toward the end of rising, preheat oven to 425 degrees.

6. In a small bowl whisk together the egg and 2 tablespoons cold water, making an egg wash. Mix thoroughly, making sure to break apart the white to achieve an even consistency. Brush rolls with egg wash, and sprinkle with sesame seeds.

7. Bake for 15 minutes, or until rolls are golden brown. Transfer to a cooling rack to cool.

Soft Baguettes and Pub Buns

One of my favorite things about this dough is its versatility. Whether you're making soft baguettes for crostini, the perfect sub sandwich, or large dinner rolls, this dough can provide just what you need. With lots of flavor, this is a great go-to for an everyday bread. I'm also a firm believer that a burger bun isn't just a vehicle for meat and other ingredients. It's an opportunity to enhance the overall flavor by giving everything a strong, flavorful foundation. Whether you want full-size buns or sliders, use this as your go-to bun recipe.

INGREDIENTS

2 1/2 cups warm water

2 tablespoons active dry yeast

2 to 2 1/2 pounds bread flour

2 tablespoons kosher salt

1/3 cup white sugar

1/3 cup canola oil

2 tablespoons distilled white vinegar

1 large egg

2 tablespoons water

Yield: 3 loaves or 24 pub buns

Prep time: 30 minutes

Inactive time: 2 hours

Bake time: 25 to 30 minutes for baguettes, 15 to 20 minutes for pub buns

Time: 3 1/2 hours

DIRECTIONS

1. In a 4-cup measuring cup, add warm water (no hotter than 115 degrees) to yeast and mix together with a whisk. Allow to sit undisturbed for approximately 10 minutes. You are looking for foam to form on the water.

2. While yeast is proofing, add flour, salt, sugar, oil, and vinegar into the bowl of an electric mixer fitted with the dough hook attachment. Once yeast has become foamy, add to flour mixture, and mix on low speed until dough comes together. If dough is not pulling away from the sides of the bowl, add a little more flour 1 tablespoon at a time until it does. When dough pulls away from the sides of the bowl, stop mixing, and wait 10 minutes for dough to hydrate.

3. Using mixer, knead dough just until it pulls away from sides of bowl. Turn out dough into a large greased bowl, and cover with plastic wrap. Allow to rise for 1 hour or until dough doubles in size. This will take less time in warmer conditions and more time in colder conditions.

RECIPE CONTINUES

4. In a small bowl whisk together the egg and water, making an egg wash.

5. To form pub buns, turn out dough onto a clean surface. Using a bench scraper to separate, divide dough into 3.5-ounce sections. Form the balls into smooth buns. First, tuck all of the slack dough to the middle, creating a smooth outer surface. Be sure that it doesn't stretch to the point of tearing. Then place the seam side down, and rotate the ball on a clean surface, dragging the bottom of the ball against the work surface to create a tight seal. Alternately, you can pinch it together creating a smooth bottom. Place the rolls 2 inches apart on a baking sheet lined with parchment. Allow to rise for 1 hour or until doubled in size. Right before baking, slash the tops of the dinner rolls with a lâme or sharp paring knife, and brush with egg wash.

6. To form baguettes, turn dough out onto a clean surface. Divide dough into three even pieces and pre-form into smooth balls. Allow to rest for 10 minutes. This will give the gluten time to relax and more flavor to develop. Turn dough upside down so the sticky side is up. Using your knuckles, start to press the air out of the dough and into a slight oval shape. Pull the top edge to the middle of the dough and press down with your fingertips to seal in place. Turn the dough 180 degrees and repeat by pulling the edge to the middle again. Now fold the dough in half toward you and use the heel of your hand to press the two edges together against the table, creating a log. Roll the short log into an 18 to 24-inch snake, pressing downward, but without stretching outward to avoid tearing. Make a second pass to lengthen. Locate the seam along the length of the baguette and make sure it's on the bottom of the loaf. Press the baguette into cornmeal and place on a baking sheet. Repeat the process with the other two loaves. Allow to rise until doubled in size.

7. Place an oven-proof dish containing 1 to 2 inches of water in the oven to create a steam bath. Ten minutes before bread has fully risen, preheat oven to 400 degrees. Bake baguettes for 25 to 30 minutes. Bake pub buns for 15 to 20 minutes. If using two sheet trays, rotate the trays after 10 minutes to ensure even browning.

Caramelized Onion and Pancetta Twist

This simple dough proves that it's what's on the inside that counts. Filled with caramelized onions, pancetta, and sun-dried tomatoes, this bread can be enjoyed with pastas, soups, or even as a sandwich. The bread is designed to be torn apart and enjoyed family style, but it will also slice nicely too. In this recipe I use aged white cheddar for its added tartness, but Fontina or even mozzarella can be substituted as well.

INGREDIENTS

1 3/4 cups warm water

2 tablespoons active dry yeast

5 cups all-purpose flour

1 tablespoon kosher salt

2 tablespoons butter, melted

3 cups shredded aged white cheddar, divided

FILLING

1 tablespoon salted butter

1 tablespoon olive oil

1 medium onion, sliced into half-rings

kosher salt

fresh cracked black pepper

2 cloves garlic, minced

4 ounces pancetta, finely diced

1 teaspoon fresh thyme leaves

1/4 cup sun-dried tomatoes in oil, chopped

DIRECTIONS

1. In a 2-cup measuring cup, add warm water (no hotter than 115 degrees) to yeast and mix together with a whisk. Allow to sit undisturbed for approximately 10 minutes. You're looking for foam to form on the water.

2. While yeast is proofing, add flour and salt into the bowl of an electric mixer with the dough hook attachment. Once yeast has become foamy, add to flour mixture. Combine all ingredients with mixer on low just until dough pulls away from the sides. Do not overmix. Allow dough to sit on mixer undisturbed for 10 minutes and hydrate. Turn mixer on low again for 1 minute. Remove bowl from mixer, and cover with plastic wrap, allowing dough to rise for 1 hour or until doubled.

3. To prepare the filling, melt the butter and olive oil in a large skillet over medium-low heat. Add onions, sprinkle with a little salt and pepper, and cook until soft and translucent. Stir regularly to prevent burning or browning too much.

RECIPE CONTINUES

Add the garlic and pancetta, and cook until pancetta is a bit crispy. Add thyme, sun-dried tomatoes, and salt and pepper to taste. Remove from heat and allow to cool while the dough finishes rising.

4. Turn out dough onto lightly floured surface, and form into a smooth oval. Cover with a tea towel and allow to rest undisturbed for 5 minutes.

5. Flatten dough using your hands, pressing it into a rectangular shape. Using a rolling pin, roll dough into a 12 x 24-inch rectangle. Make sure you don't roll too thin or braiding and forming will be challenging. Brush dough with melted butter, being sure to leave the top edge dry. Spread caramelized onion mixture over butter, and spread 3/4 of the cheese over the onions, making sure not to overfill dough.

6. To form, begin rolling dough from the bottom edge toward the top edge, tugging slightly as you go to make sure roll is fairly tight. Using a rotary cutter (pizza cutter) or knife, cut the roll in half, end to end, as evenly as you can so each half falls open. Lay one half over the other creating an X. Twist each side twice and pinch the ends. Curve the twist into a circular shape with one end longer than the other. Tuck the longer end under the circle and press in the center to seal. Sprinkle remaining cheese on top of the loaf after it's formed. Place each completed roundabout on a baking sheet lined with parchment paper at least 3 inches apart to allow for rising and baking.

7. Adjust rack in oven to middle. Preheat oven to 375 degrees approximately halfway through rise time to ensure oven is very hot. Ten minutes prior to baking, place an oven-proof dish with 1 to 2 inches of water in the oven to create a steam bath.

8. Bake bread for 15 minutes until cheese is golden brown and dough bounces back when pressed. If it doesn't, add 2 to 3 more minutes.

9. Remove carefully from oven and place on a cooling rack to cool.

Yield: 1 loaf

Prep time: 3 hours

Bake time: 25 to 30 minutes

Note: When adding the onion mixture to the dough, be sure to add the oil, as the dough will absorb it as it's cooking.

Flatbread Cooking Techniques

There are subtle differences between flatbread and pizza. Typically, flatbread is made with unleavened dough or is more cracker thin, and a pizza has a thicker, chewier crust. Another difference is baking method. In this recipe you have two options: oven or grill. For the oven method, parbake the dough on a baking sheet prior to adding toppings. For the grill method, brush the dough with olive oil and parbake directly on the grill and flip prior to adding toppings. Oven baking will yield a more pizza-like consistency while the grill will yield a more cracker-like texture and have a bit of char. For this reason, I prefer the grill method, as it creates a more complex flavor and a crisper crust. The added bonus is that my kitchen stays cooler in the summer months.

In either case, you're going to want to make sure all of your toppings have been prepared beforehand or while the dough is rising. If you're using steak, chicken, sausage, or another meat, you will want to make sure this is properly cooked before you begin the flatbread-making process. If you have leftover meat from another meal, this is a great way to use it up.

INSTRUCTIONS:

1. Make the dough on page 65 or 68.
2. Prep all of your toppings while the dough is rising.

OVEN PREPARATION:

1. Prepare a baking sheet with a piece of parchment or heat baking stone to 425 degrees in the oven.
2. Brush the top of the dough with olive oil and bake for 10 minutes.
3. Remove from heat, add toppings, and return to oven for 10 to 15 minutes or until crust is golden brown and cheese is melted.

GRILL PREPARATION:

1. Make sure your grill is very clean. The dough will be baked directly on the grill.
2. Set oven to medium indirect heat. When the grill reaches 425 degrees, brush dough with olive oil and flip onto grill, oil side down. Close grill and allow to bake for 3 to 5 minutes or until dough bubbles and bottom of crust is well browned.

3. Brush the top of the dough with olive oil, flip, and immediately add toppings to flatbread. Turn grill down to medium-low heat, and close lid. Allow to cook for about 5 to 7 minutes or until cheese is melted and begins to brown slightly. Move flatbread to a large cutting board or baking sheet using pizza peel or a couple of large spatulas. Allow to cool slightly before cutting and serving.

Pear, Pancetta, and Blue Cheese Flatbread

The sweetness of pear is balanced with the earthiness of the blue cheese on this truly magical flatbread.

INGREDIENTS

1/2 ounce active dry yeast

1 3/4 cups warm water

1 pound 6 ounces all-purpose flour

1/2 ounce kosher salt

1 tablespoon olive oil

TOPPINGS

4 ounces pancetta

1 red onion, sliced into half rings

kosher salt

2 tablespoons butter

1/4 cup dry white wine

2 springs fresh thyme

4 ounces shredded Fontina

1 Bosc pear, sliced thinly

crumbled blue cheese

arugula

balsamic vinegar reduction

olive oil

DIRECTIONS

1. To make the dough, in a 2-cup measuring cup, proof yeast by adding warm water (no hotter than 115 degrees) to yeast and mixing together with a whisk. Allow to stand undisturbed for approximately 10 minutes. You're looking for foam to form on the water.

2. While yeast is proofing, add flour and salt into the bowl of an electric mixer fitted with the dough hook attachment. Once yeast has become foamy, add to flour mixture. Add olive oil. Combine all ingredients with mixer on low just until dough pulls away from the sides. Do not overmix. Allow dough to sit on mixer undisturbed for 10 minutes and hydrate.

3. Turn mixer on low again for 1 minute. Remove bowl from mixer, and cover with plastic wrap, allowing dough to rise for 1 hour, or until doubled. Use this time to prep your filling ingredients.

4. Preheat oven to 425 degrees.

5. To prepare the toppings, finely dice the pancetta, and render fat in a large skillet on medium-low heat, stirring occasionally. Once the pancetta is crisp, move to a small bowl.

RECIPE CONTINUES

6. Leaving the rendered fat in the skillet, add onions over low heat, and sprinkle with salt. Stir occasionally to prevent browning or burning as that will make the onions bitter. Add a little butter as needed to prevent the onions from sticking to the pan. As the onions become translucent, add the white wine, and reduce until thick and syrupy. Remove from heat and allow to cool before adding to the pizza.

7. Remove the leaves from the sprigs of thyme, discarding the stems.

8. Turn out dough onto lightly floured surface. Split dough in half, and form into smooth ovals. If you want to make smaller flatbreads, you can split into four ovals. Cover dough with a tea towel and allow to rest undisturbed for 10 minutes.

9. Roll one ball of dough a couple inches smaller than the baking sheet. Line the baking sheet with parchment and transfer the dough to the sheet. Press the dough in the center, leaving a 1-inch border around the dough. Dimple the interior so it doesn't bubble. Brush with olive oil and bake for 10 minutes.

10. Remove from oven, brush with olive oil again, and top with Fontina, pear slices, caramelized onions, pancetta, and blue cheese. Bake for another 10 to 15 minutes, or until cheese is melted and crust is golden brown.

11. Top with arugula, thyme, and a drizzle of balsamic vinegar reduction. Cut into wedges or squares using rotary blade or sharp knife. Serve immediately.

Yield: 4 flatbreads

Prep time: 1 hour

Inactive time: 2 hours

Bake time: 20 to 25 minutes

Margherita Flatbread

Similar to a pizza, this Margherita flatbread is made with San Marzano tomatoes, fresh mozzarella, and fresh basil. The key to making these correctly is being sure not to add too much sauce and patting the mozzarella dry before adding it to the flatbread. Otherwise, the pizza has a tendency to get a bit soggy.

INGREDIENTS

½ ounce active dry yeast

1 ¾ cups warm water

4 ½ cups all-purpose flour

½ ounce kosher salt

2 tablespoons olive oil

¼ cup semolina flour (for the baking sheet)

SAUCE

1 can San Marzano tomatoes, pureed

3 cloves garlic, minced

1 teaspoon olive oil

½ teaspoon kosher salt

fresh cracked black pepper

TOPPINGS

fresh mozzarella (cubed, not packed in water)

fresh basil leaves

Parmesan cheese

crushed red pepper flakes

DIRECTIONS

1. In a 2-cup measuring cup, proof yeast by adding warm water (no hotter than 115 degrees) to yeast and mixing together with a whisk. Allow to stand undisturbed for approximately 10 minutes. You're looking for foam to form on the water.

2. While yeast is proofing, add flour and salt into the bowl of an electric mixer fitted with the dough hook attachment. Once yeast has become foamy add to flour mixture. Add olive oil. Combine all ingredients with mixer on low just until dough pulls away from the sides. Do not overmix. Allow dough to sit on mixer undisturbed for 10 minutes and hydrate. Turn mixer on low again for 1 minute. Remove bowl from mixer, and cover with plastic wrap, allowing dough to rise for 1 hour, or until doubled.

3. Preheat oven to 550 degrees, or your oven's hottest setting.

4. As the oven is heating, prepare the sauce and toppings. In a small bowl combine the tomatoes, garlic, olive oil, salt, and black pepper. Using a paper towel, pat the mozzarella cubes dry to remove excess moisture. Place in a second small

RECIPE CONTINUES

bowl and set aside. Remove the basil leaves from the stems and grate the Parmesan.

5. Turn out dough onto lightly floured surface. Split dough into four pieces, and form into smooth balls. Cover all with a tea towel and allow to rest for 10 minutes.

6. Roll 1 ball of dough into a 12 to 15-inch oval. Dough should be very thin. Sprinkle baking sheet with semolina, and transfer dough to pan. Brush the dough lightly with olive oil. Add tomato sauce to center of dough, leaving a ½-inch border around edges. Use the back of a spoon to spread evenly. Lightly sprinkle Parmesan over the sauce. Add a quarter of the cubed mozzarella

evenly over the entire flatbread. Tear a few of the basil leaves, and add to the top of the flatbread, distributing evenly.

7. Bake for 7 to 8 minutes, or until the crust is golden and the cheese is bubbling and browned.

8. Remove from oven, top with more fresh basil, Parmesan, and crushed red pepper flakes. Cut into wedges or squares using rotary blade or sharp knife and serve immediately.

Yield: 4 flatbreads

Prep time: 1 hour

Inactive time: 2 hours

Bake time: 7 to 8 minutes each

Sweet Breads

Edible Nostalgia

Growing up, Christmas morning traditions were the same every year. They usually started the evening before with a single gift: handmade pajamas from Gramma. Our second gift was set by our bed to open in the morning. We knew they were slippers, but it always kept us in our room long enough for Mom and Dad to get downstairs to get breakfast started. We weren't allowed to leave our rooms until we smelled coffee brewing and heard Mom ask Dad if he remembered to check the batteries in the camera.

"Can we come out yet?" Bryan would bellow from his open bedroom door. If ever there was a kid who feared missing out, it was my little brother. With each passing moment, he would army-crawl a few inches down the hall until Dad would give the okay. It was as if he believed the gifts would disappear if he didn't get downstairs fast enough to claim them.

At the base of the stairs, we had to pose for our annual Christmas morning picture, pajamas wrinkled and hair disheveled—another one for the family album. Each year, I remember thinking no one would ever want to see those photos, but now I much prefer them to our rigidly posed school photos.

The fragrance of spices and butter began to fill the air; the cinnamon rolls were almost ready. We had just enough time to open our stockings before we could dig in to breakfast. Presents could wait for cinnamon rolls. It's challenging to open gifts when you're salivating.

There's something so incredibly heartwarming and nostalgic about cinnamon rolls. Whether you too always had them on Christmas morning, or a trip to the county fair was never completed without one, they seem to be a fairly common tradition. When I opened the bakery, I knew it was something I wanted to offer and create as a tradition for our new community since we were the only bakery in town.

I knew I had a challenge ahead of me. As a self-proclaimed connoisseur of cinnamon rolls, I'd had great ones and not-so-great ones. How could I create the perfect cinnamon roll that my inner child remembered from Christmas morning? Something that had complex flavor and wasn't so sweet that it couldn't be finished before the center was reached? It's still a cardinal sin to throw away the center of a cinnamon roll. Ask anyone, they'll tell you.

I determined that a truly good cinnamon roll could stand alone without any frosting at all. It wasn't something to mask dryness or lack of flavor. Besides, when they were first created in Sweden, they weren't frosted. That became my own personal bar of excellence. I decided to break it down into all of the elements.

I determined that a truly good cinnamon roll could stand alone without any frosting at all.

First, the dough had to have a really nice flavor and texture. I wasn't about to leave it up to the filling to do all of the work. The dough had to be able to stand on its own as a loaf of bread. Soft and chewy in texture, yeasty tasting and with a little tang. All good things are built upon a strong foundation.

Next was creating a filling that was sweet, but more importantly had depth of flavor. White sugar was not invited to this flavor party. Dark brown sugar and dark honey are both sweet and also contribute their unique earthiness. Vanilla extract adds faux sweetness along with its slightly floral notes. While there are a few different kinds of cinnamon, Saigon reigns supreme in both quality and flavor. Lastly, only salted sweet cream butter would do for the perfect roll. One of the greatest disappointments I've had with a cinnamon roll is dryness. I concluded that part of the reason some rolls were so dry is because there just wasn't enough butter to be absorbed into the dough as it baked. Rather than brush on melted butter, it only seemed right to whip everything together into a fluffy paste and schmear it on the dough like frosting. I will never do it differently.

Finally, the perfect cinnamon roll should have a crown of cream cheese frosting. Not icing that's diluted in both texture and flavor, but an honest-to-goodness cake frosting that's good enough for red velvet. It would be spread over the swirls of cinnamon straight out of the oven so it could melt down between each layer before it's served.

Whether you've had one of our rolls at the bakery or making them at home will be your first experience, I hope these will bring back happy memories and help you to create new ones.

The Ultimate Cinnamon Rolls

When I think of the perfect cinnamon roll, I think of dough with a great flavor and texture, not too sweet, but with robust cinnamon filling and a cream cheese frosting befitting any cake. The ultimate indulgence!

INGREDIENTS

2 tablespoons active dry yeast

2 1/2 cups warm water

2 to 2 1/2 pounds bread flour

2 tablespoons kosher salt

1/3 cup white sugar

1/3 cup canola oil

2 tablespoons distilled white vinegar

Cinnamon Filling (page 169)

Cream Cheese Frosting (page 159)

Yield: 1 dozen cinnamon rolls

Prep time: 1 hour

Inactive time: 2 hours

Bake time: 20 to 22 minutes

Time: 3 1/2 hours

DIRECTIONS

1. In a 4-cup measuring cup, proof yeast by adding warm water (no hotter than 115 degrees) to yeast and mixing together with a whisk. Allow to sit undisturbed for approximately 10 minutes. You are looking for foam to form on the water.

2. While yeast is proofing, add flour, salt, sugar, oil, and vinegar into the bowl of an electric mixer fitted with the dough hook attachment. Once yeast has become foamy, add to flour mixture, and mix on low speed until dough comes together. If dough is not pulling away from the sides of the bowl, add a little more flour at a time until it does. Once dough pulls away cleanly from the sides of the bowl, stop mixing and wait 10 minutes for dough to hydrate.

3. Using the mixer, knead dough just until it pulls away from sides of bowl. Turn out dough into a large greased bowl, and cover with plastic wrap. Allow to rise for 1 hour or until dough doubles in size. This will take less time in warmer conditions and more time in colder conditions.

4. Take this time to make cinnamon filling on page 169.

RECIPE CONTINUES

5. Turn out dough onto floured surface. Gently form into an oval. Dough should be horizontal to you so as you roll, you'll end up with a horizontal rectangle. Pat dough flat with your hands first to release the air. Roll dough into a rectangle, correcting as necessary until dough measures approximately 30 inches wide and 20 inches tall. Spread filling over dough using spatula (or bowl scraper), taking care to leave 1 inch along the top edge clean so it will seal when rolled.

6. Begin rolling the dough into a tight coil, starting at one corner and working across. When you get to the other end, work back the other way, tugging lightly as you go to ensure the roll is tight. Continue this pattern until you reach the top. Pull the top edge over, stretching slightly and sealing it to the rest of the roll. Stretch the long roll a bit to even out any thick areas.

7. Preheat oven to 400 degrees. Using a sharp knife, trim the two ends of the dough and discard. Then measure and cut the roll in half. Cut each half in half so you have four equal sections. Cut each of those sections into thirds so you have twelve equal rolls. Carefully transfer rolls to three 8 x 8-inch pans that have been sprayed with nonstick spray. Cover with plastic wrap and allow to rise until rolls double in size (approximately 15 to 20 minutes).

8. Bake for 20 to 22 minutes, or until tops are golden brown and bounce back when pressed lightly.

Tips:

1. Rolling out the dough into a rectangle can be tricky. If you find that as you are rolling, your dough tends to resist rolling easily, it's letting you know it is overworked. Allow it to rest for 2 minutes, and then continue rolling. The gluten in the dough should be relaxed enough to cooperate.

2. As you're rolling up the dough into the log shape, you may find that it begins to roll unevenly like a rug sometimes does. Stretch the unrolled dough even with the rolled part and continue rolling up.

3. If you find that your log is thicker in some parts and thinner in others, you can stretch the log longer to thin out the thicker parts, or bunch up in the areas that are thinner. This will help you achieve a more consistent thickness throughout.

Pineapple Upside-Down Cinnamon Rolls

What happens when you combine the nostalgia of a pineapple upside-down cake and the classic cinnamon roll is nothing short of pure magic. The acidity and fruitiness of the pineapple balances the spicy sweetness of the cinnamon and brown sugar, creating an exciting marriage of two iconic desserts.

INGREDIENTS

1 pound 10 ounces all-purpose flour

$1/2$ teaspoon ground nutmeg

1 tablespoon kosher salt

1 tablespoon active dry yeast

$1/2$ cup white sugar

$1/4$ cup ($1/2$ stick) salted butter, cubed and softened

2 large eggs, room temperature

$2/3$ cup warm water

1 cup whole milk, warmed

FILLING

Cinnamon Filling (page 169)

2 cans sliced pineapples

1 small jar maraschino cherries

$1/4$ cup ($1/2$ stick) butter, melted

1 cup dark brown sugar

$1/4$ cup pineapple juice

1 teaspoon vanilla extract

DIRECTIONS

1. Add flour, nutmeg, salt, yeast, and sugar into the bowl of an electric mixer fitted with the dough hook attachment and combine. Add butter cubes to flour mixture and mix for 2 minutes.

2. Add eggs, water (no hotter than 115 degrees), and milk, and combine until dough is soft and stretchy and there are no lumps of butter. Add more flour if necessary so dough will pull away from sides of bowl.

3. Let rest for 5 to 10 minutes until you can see some rise. In the mixer, knead for 1 minute until dough pulls away from sides again. Turn out dough into a greased container to rise until doubled in size. Form the dough into an oval. Let dough rest for 5 minutes before rolling out.

4. Make the cinnamon filling on page 169.

5. Prepare three 8 x 8-inch baking pans. If you're using disposable pans, place on a baking sheet for stability and to catch drips. Spray with nonstick spray, and put four pineapple rounds, two by two, in each tray. Place a maraschino cherry in the center of each pineapple round.

RECIPE CONTINUES

6. Roll out dough into a large rectangle, approximately 30 inches wide by 24 inches. Fill with cinnamon filling, leaving a 1-inch bare strip along top edge to seal. Roll tightly and seal by pinching dough together.

7. Make sure that the thickness of the roll is consistent throughout the entire length by stretching or bunching dough. Using a sharp knife, trim ends with a rock-and-lift motion. Cut the roll in half. Then cut each half in half again to get quarters. Then cut each piece into thirds to get 12 rolls total. Place each roll directly on top of the pineapple rounds.

8. Whisk together the melted butter, brown sugar, pineapple juice, and vanilla in a small bowl, and scoop over each of the cinnamon rolls, spreading so it drips down the sides.

9. Allow the rolls to rise for 30 minutes. Place an oven-proof dish containing 1 to 2 inches of water on the bottom rack of the oven to create a steam bath. Preheat the oven to 375 degrees the last 10 minutes before the rolls are ready to bake.

10. When rolls have finished rising, bake for 25 to 35 minutes. Allow to cool for 10 minutes, and carefully turn rolls out of their pans onto another baking sheet. Be careful to ensure pineapples stay on top of each of the cinnamon rolls when removed from pan. Serve immediately.

Yield: 12 cinnamon rolls

Prep time: 30 minutes

Inactive time: 2 hours

Bake time: 20 to 25 minutes

Apple Streusel Cinnamon Rolls

If an apple streusel pie married a cinnamon roll, this would be their happily ever after. Tart apples balance the sweetness of the ultimate cinnamon roll crowned with a crumbly streusel.

INGREDIENTS

2 ½ cups warm water

2 tablespoons active dry yeast

2 to 2 ½ pounds bread flour

2 tablespoons kosher salt

6 tablespoons white sugar

⅓ cup canola oil

2 tablespoons distilled white vinegar

APPLE FILLING

Cinnamon Filling (page 169)

2 Granny Smith apples, peeled and diced

¼ cup brown sugar

1 teaspoon ground cinnamon

¼ teaspoon ground cloves

¼ teaspoon ground ginger

¼ teaspoon ground nutmeg

CINNAMON CRUMBLE

1 cup dark brown sugar

½ cup all-purpose flour

¼ cup (½ stick) butter, melted

1 teaspoon ground cinnamon

DIRECTIONS

1. In a 4-cup measuring cup, proof yeast by adding warm water (no hotter than 115 degrees) to yeast and mixing together with a whisk. Allow to sit undisturbed for approximately 10 minutes. You're looking for foam to form on the water.

2. While yeast is proofing, add flour, salt, sugar, oil, and vinegar into the bowl of an electric mixer fitted with the dough hook attachment. Once yeast has become foamy, add to flour mixture, and mix on low speed until dough comes together. If dough is not pulling away from the sides of the bowl, add a little more flour at a time until it does. Once dough pulls away from the sides, stop mixer and wait 10 minutes for dough to hydrate.

3. Using mixer, knead dough just until it pulls away from sides of bowl. Turn out dough into a large greased bowl, and cover with plastic wrap. Allow to rise for 1 hour or until dough doubles in size. This will take less time in warmer conditions and more time in colder conditions.

4. Make cinnamon filling on page 169.

5. Peel and dice Granny Smith apples, and toss with brown sugar, cinnamon, cloves, ginger, and nutmeg in a separate bowl.

RECIPE CONTINUES

 79

6. In another bowl make the cinnamon crumble by mixing together brown sugar, flour, melted butter, and cinnamon.

7. Turn out dough onto floured surface. And gently form into an oval. Dough should be horizontal to you, so as you roll, you'll end up with a horizontal rectangle. Pat dough flat with your hands first to release the air. Create a valley in the middle of the dough along the length of the dough. Then begin to roll side to side starting from the middle (once each way), and then roll toward you and away from you, starting at the middle point. Try to maintain the rectangular shape, correcting as necessary until dough measures approximately 30 inches wide by 20 inches. The more even your rectangle, the more equal each cinnamon roll will be.

8. Spread cinnamon filling over dough using spatula (or bowl scraper), taking care to leave 1 inch along the top edge clean so it will seal when rolled. Sprinkle apples over cinnamon filling. Begin rolling the dough into a tight coil, starting at one corner and working across. When you get to the other end, work back the other way, tugging lightly as you go to ensure the roll is tight. Continue this pattern until you reach the top. Pull the top edge over, stretching slightly and sealing it to the rest of the roll. Stretch the long roll a bit to even out any thick areas.

9. Using a sharp knife, trim the two ends and discard. Then measure and cut the roll in half. Cut each half in half so you have four equal sections. Cut each of those sections into thirds so you have twelve equal rolls. Carefully transfer rolls to three 8 x 8-inch baking pans that have been sprayed with nonstick spray. Liberally sprinkle cinnamon crumble over the rolls. Cover with plastic wrap and allow to rise approximately 15 to 20 minutes.

10. Place an oven-proof dish containing 1 to 2 inches of water on the bottom rack of the oven to create a steam bath. Preheat oven to 400 degrees. Bake for 20 to 22 minutes. Allow to cool 10 minutes before serving.

Yield: 12 rolls

Prep time: 30 minutes

Inactive time: 2 hours

Bake time: 20 minutes

Cream Cheese Rolls

Cream cheese frosting is great for many things (namely cake, cinnamon rolls, and even as a midnight snack with a spoon), but what if you baked the frosting into a cinnamon roll, but without the cinnamon? This was a thought I had early one morning at the bakery, and after the first dozen came out of the oven, it was clear these were going to be super addictive. Customers soon dubbed them "crack rolls," and they more than stand up to their name. The key to making these easier to construct is to have cold frosting. Not so cold that it's completely impossible to spread, but cold enough that it's not slippery. A fine line that will make all the difference.

INGREDIENTS

Cream Cheese Frosting (page 159), cold

2 tablespoons active dry yeast

2 1/2 cups warm water

2 to 2 1/2 pounds bread flour

2 tablespoons kosher salt

6 tablespoons white sugar

1/3 cup canola oil

2 tablespoons distilled white vinegar

powdered sugar

Yield: 12 cinnamon rolls

Prep Time: 30 minutes

Inactive time: 2 hours

Bake Time: 20 to 22 minutes

DIRECTIONS

1. Start by making cream cheese frosting (recipe on page 159), and place in the freezer for approximately 20 minutes. You can also make it the day before, refrigerate overnight, and take out before you begin to make the dough.

2. In a 4-cup measuring cup, proof yeast by adding warm water (no hotter than 115 degrees) to yeast and mixing together with a whisk. Allow to sit undisturbed for approximately 10 minutes. You're looking for foam to form on the water.

3. While yeast is proofing, add flour, salt, sugar, oil, and vinegar to the bowl of an electric mixer fitted with the dough hook attachment. Once yeast has become foamy, add to flour mixture, and mix on low speed until dough comes together. If dough is not pulling away from the sides of the bowl, add a little more flour at a time until it does. Once dough pulls away from the sides, stop mixer and wait 10 minutes for dough to hydrate.

RECIPE CONTINUES

4. Using the mixer, knead dough just until it pulls away from sides of bowl. Turn out dough into a large greased bowl, and cover with plastic wrap. Allow to rise for 1 hour or until dough doubles in size. This will take less time in warmer conditions and more time in colder conditions.

5. Turn out dough onto floured surface, and gently form into an oval. Dough should be horizontal to you, so as you roll, you'll end up with a horizontal rectangle. Pat dough flat with your hands first to release the air. Create a valley in the middle of the dough along the length of the dough. Then begin to roll side to side starting from the middle (once each way), and then roll toward you and away from you, starting at the middle point. Try to maintain the rectangular shape, correcting as necessary until dough measures approximately 30 inches wide by 20 inches. The more even your rectangle, the more equal each cinnamon roll will be.

6. Spread frosting over dough using spatula (or bowl scraper), taking care to leave 1 inch along the top edge clean so it will seal when rolled.

7. Begin rolling the dough into a tight coil, starting at one corner and working across. When you get to the other end, work back the other way, tugging lightly as you go to ensure the roll is tight. Continue this pattern until you reach the top. Pull the top edge over, stretching slightly and sealing it to the rest of the roll. Stretch the long roll a bit to even out any thick areas.

8. Fill a small oven-safe dish with water to create steam, and place on the bottom rack. Preheat oven to 400 degrees.

9. Using a sharp knife, trim the two ends of the dough and discard. Then measure and cut the roll in half. Cut each half in half so you have four equal sections. Cut each of those sections into thirds so you have twelve equal rolls. Carefully transfer rolls to three 8 x 8-inch baking pans that have been sprayed with nonstick spray. Cover with plastic wrap and allow to rise approximately 15 to 20 minutes.

10. Bake for 22 minutes, or until tops are golden brown and bounce back when pressed lightly. Using a sifter, sprinkle powdered sugar over the tops of the rolls and serve warm.

Maple Pecan Cinnamon Rolls

Pure maple syrup and chopped pecans take the
ultimate cinnamon rolls to the next level.

INGREDIENTS

2 tablespoons active dry yeast

2 1/2 cups warm water

2 to 2 1/2 pounds bread flour

2 tablespoons kosher salt

1/3 cup white sugar

1/3 cup canola oil

2 tablespoons distilled white
   vinegar

FILLING

1 cup (2 sticks) butter,
   softened

2 cups dark brown sugar

1/4 cup pure maple extract

1/4 cup ground cinnamon

1 tablespoon vanilla extract

1 cup pecans, chopped

ICING

1/4 cup pure maple syrup

1 cup powdered sugar

1/4 teaspoon pure maple extract

DIRECTIONS

1. In a 4-cup measuring cup, proof yeast by adding
    warm water (no hotter than 115 degrees) to yeast
    and mixing together with a whisk. Allow to sit
    undisturbed for approximately 10 minutes. You
    are looking for foam to form on the water.

2. While yeast is proofing, add flour, salt, sugar, oil,
    and vinegar to the bowl of an electric mixer fitted
    with the dough hook attachment. Once yeast has
    become foamy, add to flour mixture, and mix on
    low speed until dough comes together. If dough is
    not pulling away from the sides of the bowl, add
    a little more flour at a time until it does. Once
    dough pulls away cleanly from the sides of the
    bowl, stop mixing and wait 10 minutes for dough
    to hydrate.

3. Using the mixer, knead dough just until it pulls
    away from sides of bowl. Turn out dough into a
    large greased bowl, and cover with plastic wrap.
    Allow to rise for 1 hour or until dough doubles
    in size. This will take less time in warmer
    conditions and more time in colder conditions.

4. Take this time to make cinnamon roll filling in
    your electric mixer.

RECIPE CONTINUES

5. Turn out dough onto floured surface. Gently form into an oval. Dough should be horizontal to you, so as you roll, you'll end up with a horizontal rectangle. Pat dough flat with your hands first to release the air. Roll dough into a rectangle, correcting as necessary until dough measures approximately 30 inches wide by 20 inches. Spread filling over dough using spatula (or bowl scraper), taking care to leave 1 inch along the top edge clean so it will seal when rolled.

6. Begin rolling the dough into a tight coil, starting at one corner and working across. When you get to the other end, work back the other way, tugging lightly as you go to ensure the roll is tight. Continue this pattern until you reach the top. Pull the top edge over, stretching slightly and sealing it to the rest of the roll. Stretch the long roll a bit to even out any thick areas.

7. Preheat oven to 400 degrees. Using a sharp knife, trim the two ends and discard. Then measure and cut the roll in half. Cut each half in half so you have 4 equal sections. Cut each of those sections into thirds so you have 12 equal rolls. Carefully transfer rolls to three 8 x 8-inch pans that have been sprayed with nonstick spray. Cover with plastic wrap and allow to rise until rolls double in size (approximately 15 to 20 minutes). Bake for 20 to 22 minutes, or until tops are golden brown and bounce back when pressed lightly.

Yield: 12 cinnamon rolls

Prep time: 45 minutes

Inactive time: 2 hours

Bake time: 20 to 22 minutes

Time: 3 1/2 hours

The Language of Food

After we pulled up to the sky-blue 1950s ranch-style home in Anaheim for a birthday party, where a bounce house and balloons filled most of the front yard, Eva took the gift she'd made for her friend Ariana into the house and then disappeared into the giant castle, kicking off her shoes on the way. We appeared to be early, even though the invitation said noon and it was five after. I stood alone awkwardly in the empty living room, waiting to introduce myself to one of the birthday girl's parents.

"Come on out back!" someone called out from beyond the sliding glass door.

I hadn't intended to stay, but as I headed into the backyard, I saw the long rows of tables, and Ariana's dad was filling coolers with ice and drinks. Fruit trees lined the back fence, and colorful garland shined brightly against a cloudless spring sky. Under the awning, a makeshift kitchen was being set up. A scullery of sorts with a griddle and folding tables held bowls of ingredients and big batches of salsa. Busy women in aprons bustled about, organizing their workstations and speaking a language I only vaguely remembered from high school classes.

Ariana's dad introduced me to his mom, aunts, and abuela. One of his cousins was making *pupusas*, lining the griddle with what looked like a cross between a quesadilla and a tamale. With my curiosity piqued, I watched as her hands expertly worked the masa, creating flat patties filled with meat, beans, and cheese. Each one was toasted on the griddle just long enough to brown each side. She handed me a plate and motioned to the plastic forks and salsa. I loaded up my plate and sat down with a few women who had arrived.

"Have you had food from El Salvador before?" one of them asked. She worked in the school system as an English as a Second Language counselor. I can't remember how she was related to Ariana's family, but we sat and chatted about how her family ran a food stand in Los Angeles selling pupusas all week long. This food was their livelihood.

My curiosity turned into obsession, and I more intently watched their hands, analyzing their technique.

"This is my first time," I replied. "They look delicious! I can't wait to try." I would be lying if I said I ate fewer than seven. Filled with pork, cheese, beans, and a kick of heat, they were truly a marriage of delicious ingredients wrapped in toasted ground corn dough. "Wow! These are pure heaven. I could eat these forever."

My curiosity turned into obsession, and I more intently watched their hands, analyzing their technique. By this time, they had crowded into their makeshift kitchen, and I wandered over to watch more closely, fascinated with this new food. In broken Spanish, I asked questions, trying to translate and remember their answers. Abuela stopped working and looked at me for a moment with questioning eyes, possibly pondering my interest.

What mattered more was that even with a language barrier, I had bonded with these women over their cuisine and, in turn, with a part of their culture.

I smiled at her and said, "*Es divertido, no*?" (It's fun, isn't it?)

With that, she pulled me into the makeshift kitchen and plopped fresh masa into my hand. "*Ayuda*," she commanded. "You help."

Both shocked and delighted, I followed intently as my new teacher showed me the ropes, cupping the dough in my hand, making a well for the filling. Closing the dough around it like a dumpling and then carefully patting it into a pancake before setting it on the griddle, I made the first one perfectly out of sheer luck, and she called for the others to look. A few gasped, almost as if to say, *Well, I'll be darned—she did it!* A little cheer for the new recruit and another ball of masa was placed in my hand. I was now a part of the crew. I felt like I had landed in the middle of an *I Love Lucy* episode, except I was making friends instead of a chocolatey mess. I stayed the entire afternoon and evening, helping in the kitchen until it was time to leave.

I can't tell you how many pupusas I made that day. The number doesn't really matter. What mattered more was that even with a language barrier, I had bonded with these women over their cuisine and, in turn, with a part of their culture. They didn't have to invite me in, but they did so anyway. In a way, it was another form of breaking bread. Being open to connection despite cultural differences. Fellowship over food. I don't know if I'll ever get the chance to go back and visit them, but the experience lit a fire to find more just like it. It's amazing what can happen when you throw caution to the wind and say yes.

Cinnamon Roll Bread Pudding

Similar to a French toast casserole, bread pudding is a fantastic way to use up odds and ends of breads, making it a very economical dish. On the rare occasion that we had leftover cinnamon rolls at the bakery, they made their way into this Saturday special. Whether you use cinnamon rolls, brioche, or another type of sweet bread, this will surely be a crowd pleaser.

BREAD PUDDING

4 large eggs

2 cups whole buttermilk

2 teaspoons vanilla extract

1 teaspoon ground cinnamon

1/2 teaspoon ground nutmeg

1/2 cup white sugar

2 tablespoons honey bourbon or whiskey

1/2 cups pecans, chopped (optional)

8 cups cinnamon rolls or brioche, cubed

2 tablespoons turbinado sugar

BOURBON SAUCE

1/4 cup (1/2 stick) butter

3 tablespoons heavy cream

1/2 cup dark brown sugar

2 tablespoons honey bourbon or whiskey

DIRECTIONS

1. For the bread pudding, prepare a 9 x 13-inch pan with nonstick spray.

2. In a large bowl whisk together eggs, buttermilk, vanilla, cinnamon, nutmeg, white sugar, and bourbon. Stir in pecans, and then fold in cubed cinnamon rolls or bread, coating evenly.

3. Pour bread mixture into prepared pan, cover tightly in plastic wrap, and refrigerate overnight, or at least 8 hours.

4. Preheat oven to 350 degrees. Remove bread pudding from refrigerator and remove plastic wrap. Sprinkle with turbinado sugar and bake 30 to 40 minutes.

5. To make bourbon sauce, in a saucepan over medium-low heat, combine butter, heavy cream, brown sugar, and bourbon. Simmer until thickened, stirring frequently. Remove from heat, cool slightly, and drizzle over bread pudding to serve.

Yield: One 9 x 13-inch pan

Prep time: 10 minutes

Inactive time: 8 hours

Bake time: 30 to 40 minutes

Orange Blueberry Muffins

The key to a memorable blueberry muffin is a little orange zest. While these muffins are delicious even without the zest, it adds a cheery element of surprise. Liners can be used in your pan, but I find the extra crispiness of the muffins baked in a greased pan creates an extra-toasty element.

INGREDIENTS

2 cups plus 2 tablespoons all-purpose flour, divided

1 teaspoon baking soda

1/2 teaspoon baking powder

1/2 teaspoon kosher salt

3/4 cup (1 1/2 sticks) salted butter, softened

1 1/3 cups white sugar

3 large eggs

2 teaspoons vanilla extract

1 cup Greek yogurt

zest of one orange

2 cups blueberries, divided

Yield: 18 to 20 standard-size muffins

Prep time: 15 minutes

Bake time: 18 to 20 minutes

DIRECTIONS

1. Preheat oven to 375 degrees with rack placed in the center of the oven.

2. In a large bowl mix together 2 cups flour, baking soda, baking powder, and salt with a whisk.

3. In the bowl of an electric mixer fitted with the paddle attachment, cream together butter and sugar, first on low to combine, and then on high for 5 minutes until light and fluffy. The color should be almost completely white. Scrape down sides of the bowl.

4. Add eggs one at a time, beating after each addition. Scrape sides of the bowl to check for even consistency.

5. Add vanilla, Greek yogurt, and orange zest, and mix on low until fully combined.

6. Add flour mixture and mix just until fully combined. Remove bowl from mixer and fold gently, checking for any runny spots. Texture should resemble really soft ice cream.

7. Dredge 1 1/2 cups of rinsed and drained blueberries in 2 tablespoons of flour. Gently fold dredged berries into muffin batter, taking care not to burst any berries.

RECIPE CONTINUES

8. Scoop batter into greased muffin tins. Don't overfill. You should have approximately 20 muffins. Bake for 18 to 20 minutes, or until a toothpick comes out clean.

9. Cool for 10 minutes, then move muffins to a cooling rack, and allow to cool completely before storing.

Apple Cardamom Muffins

Cardamom breaks away from the traditional, giving these apple muffins a more exotic, toasty twist. Granny Smith apples and Greek yogurt add a slight tartness, making these muffins sweet, but not too sweet.

INGREDIENTS

2 $1/4$ cups all-purpose flour

1 teaspoon baking soda

$1/2$ teaspoon baking powder

$1/2$ teaspoon kosher salt

1 teaspoon ground cinnamon

$1/4$ teaspoon ground cardamom

$1/4$ teaspoon allspice

$3/4$ cup (1 $1/2$ sticks) butter, softened

1 $1/3$ cups white sugar

3 large eggs

2 teaspoons vanilla extract

1 cup Greek yogurt

1 Granny Smith apple

CRUMBLE

1 cup dark brown sugar

$1/2$ cup all-purpose flour

$1/4$ cup ($1/2$ cup) butter, melted

1 teaspoon ground cinnamon

$1/4$ teaspoon ground cardamom

INGREDIENTS CONTINUE

DIRECTIONS

1. Preheat oven to 375 degrees with a rack placed in the center position.

2. In a large bowl whisk together flour, baking soda, baking powder, salt, cinnamon, cardamom, and allspice.

3. In the bowl of an electric mixer fitted with the paddle attachment, cream together butter and sugar first on low to combine, and then on high for 5 minutes or until light and fluffy. The color should be almost completely white. Scrape down sides.

4. In a separate bowl whisk eggs and vanilla together, then add to flour mixture. Combine on low, then mix on high. Scrape sides of the bowl to make sure mixture is fully combined.

5. Add Greek yogurt, then mix on low until combined. Peel, core, and cut apple into $1/2$-inch cubes. Add apples and mix again on low, then scrape bowl again to ensure complete mixing.

6. Add flour mixture and combine just until you don't see any more flour. Remove bowl from electric mixer, and using spatula, fold a few times, checking for even mixing. There's a fine line between overmixing and even incorporation, so don't overmix, but ensure that the texture is uniform throughout.

RECIPE CONTINUES

ICING (OPTIONAL)

apple juice

powdered sugar

7. Scoop batter into muffin tins lined with muffin cups.

8. In a bowl mix together brown sugar, flour, melted butter, cinnamon, and cardamon and sprinkle crumble on top.

9. Bake for 25 to 30 minutes until toothpick inserted in the middle comes out clean.

10. For the icing, in a small bowl mix together apple juice and powdered sugar, and drizzle over the muffins once baked and cooled. Icing should be thick enough that it doesn't run clear.

Yield: 18 muffins

Prep time: 15 minutes

Bake time: 25 to 30 minutes

Brioche French Toast with Kumquat Whipped Cream

Brioche is undeniably one of the best French toast breads there is. Buttery, soft, and sweet, it's perfection. However, the cinnamon braided brioche takes this bread to the next level. Topped with kumquat whipped cream, it's heaven on a plate.

INGREDIENTS

6 large eggs

2 cups half-and-half

1 teaspoon vanilla extract

2 tablespoons honey, warmed

1/2 teaspoon ground cinnamon

1 loaf brioche, 3/4 to 1-inch slices

1/2 cup (1 stick) butter

WHIPPED CREAM

2 cups heavy whipping cream

2 tablespoons powdered sugar

1 teaspoon vanilla extract

3 to 4 tablespoons kumquat jam or marmalade

Yield: 8 to 10 slices

Prep time: 10 minutes

Cook time: 15 to 20 minutes

DIRECTIONS

1. In a large bowl whisk together eggs, half-and-half, vanilla, honey, and cinnamon, and pour into a shallow pan. Dip bread into pan for 20 to 30 seconds on each side, allowing bread to absorb mixture.

2. Heat a large skillet or griddle over medium-low heat. Melt 2 tablespoons of butter, coating skillet evenly.

3. Add two slices at a time into the skillet, or four on a griddle, and cook until golden brown, approximately 2 to 3 minutes per side. Remove from the heat and keep warm on a rack in the oven until all the slices have been cooked. Serve immediately.

4. To make whipped cream, using either an electric or hand mixer, add cream, powdered sugar, and vanilla to a bowl, and beat until soft peaks form. Add kumquat jam and beat until peaks stiffen. Don't overmix. Serve over French toast with additional kumquat jam.

Scones, Biscuits, and Brunch

A good scone has a flaky, buttery texture. Depending on where you are in the world, a scone may appear more like an American biscuit, but I assure you they're not the same. Although made with similar ingredients, the proportions differ greatly. Scones often have eggs while biscuits do not. There are as many scone recipes as there are biscuit recipes. If you've ever visited the South, you know that biscuits are serious business and just by tweaking the same ingredients, biscuits can vary a hundred different ways.

Walnut Blue Cheese Scones

Blue cheese may not traditionally be a breakfast or brunch ingredient; however, combined with the earthiness of walnuts and the sweetness of honey or fig preserves, it creates the perfect symphony of flavor that is both savory and sweet.

INGREDIENTS

2 cups all-purpose flour

1/4 cup white sugar

1/2 teaspoon kosher salt

2 1/2 teaspoons baking powder

1/2 cup (1 stick) salted butter, frozen

1/2 cup buttermilk, cold

1 large egg

1/4 cup honey, warmed

1/2 cup walnuts, chopped finely

1 cup blue cheese, crumbled

Yield: 8 scones

Prep time: 10 minutes

Bake time: 20 to 25 minutes

DIRECTIONS

1. In a bowl whisk together flour, sugar, salt, and baking powder.

2. Grate frozen butter and toss in flour mixture. Refrigerate while preparing the rest of the ingredients.

3. In a separate bowl whisk together buttermilk, egg, and warm honey.

4. Toss the walnuts and blue cheese into the flour mixture.

5. Mix the buttermilk mixture into the flour mixture, stirring just until everything completely comes together.

6. Turn out dough onto a clean, heavily floured work surface. Flour the top of the dough, and form dough into an 8-inch disk. Cut the disk into eight equal wedges. Transfer wedges to a baking sheet lined with parchment paper. Brush with buttermilk and refrigerate for 15 minutes.

7. Preheat oven to 400 degrees. Bake scones for 20 to 25 minutes until golden brown. Allow to cool for 10 minutes before moving to a cooling rack. Serve with butter and honey or fig preserves.

Carrot Cake Scones

I love a great carrot cake. I also love a great scone. This mash-up gives you the best of both worlds. Most scone recipes call for white sugar, but I found that bringing brown sugar into the mix creates a wonderfully toasty flavor that plays really well with the carrot. Golden raisins add great flavor too, but if you're not a fan of raisins, you can replace with more walnuts. Just remember to keep the pieces small so cutting the wedges isn't challenging.

INGREDIENTS

2 1/4 cups all-purpose flour

1/4 cup brown sugar

1/4 cup white sugar

1/2 teaspoon kosher salt

2 1/2 teaspoons baking powder

1/2 teaspoon ground cinnamon

1/4 teaspoon ground nutmeg

1/2 cup (1 stick) butter, frozen

1/2 cup buttermilk, cold

1 large egg

1 1/2 teaspoons vanilla extract

1 cup shredded carrot

1/4 cup chopped walnuts

1/4 cup golden raisins

GLAZE

1 cup powdered sugar

1 to 2 tablespoons buttermilk

1/2 teaspoon vanilla

DIRECTIONS

1. In a large bowl whisk together flour, brown sugar, white sugar, salt, baking powder, nutmeg, and cinnamon.

2. Grate frozen butter and toss in the flour mixture. Refrigerate to keep cold while you prep the rest of the ingredients.

3. In a separate bowl whisk together buttermilk, egg, and vanilla.

4. Toss shredded carrot, walnuts, and raisins in flour mixture. Add buttermilk mixture to flour mixture, and stir with a spatula until almost all of the flour is worked in.

5. Turn out dough onto a clean, heavily floured work surface. Using a bench scraper, begin to fold the dough, pressing down after each fold, and flouring to keep from sticking. Form dough into an 8-inch round disk. Use bench scraper to cut disk into eight equal wedges. Transfer wedges to baking sheet lined with parchment paper. Brush wedges with buttermilk and refrigerate for 15 minutes.

RECIPE CONTINUES

Yield: 8 scones

Prep time: 10 minutes

Bake time: 20 to 25 minutes

6. Preheat oven to 400 degrees. Bake scones for 20 to 25 minutes. Allow to cool for 10 minutes before moving to a cooling rack.

7. To make glaze, in a bowl whisk together the powdered sugar, buttermilk, and vanilla. Consistency should be thick, but still pourable. Drizzle glaze over scones.

Lemon Poppyseed Scones

I love how fresh and lemony these are. With lemon zest baked into the scones and drizzled with a lemon juice icing, these pack a big punch. Using a buttery classic scone recipe, these come together super quick and will make you glad lemons are available all year long. Serve with raspberry jam for extra goodness!

INGREDIENTS

2 cups all-purpose flour

1/2 cup white sugar

1/2 teaspoon kosher salt

2 1/2 teaspoons baking powder

zest of 2 lemons

1 teaspoon poppyseeds

1/2 cup (1 stick) salted butter, frozen

1/2 cup buttermilk, cold

1 large egg

ICING

2 to 3 tablespoons fresh lemon juice

1 cup powdered sugar

DIRECTIONS

1. Preheat oven to 400 degrees. Line a baking sheet with parchment paper.

2. In a bowl whisk together flour, sugar, salt, baking powder, lemon zest, and poppyseeds. Grate frozen butter into flour mixture, toss, and set aside.

3. In a small bowl whisk together buttermilk and egg. Add to the flour mixture and stir just until it comes together. Do not overmix.

4. Pour dough onto a floured work surface. Flour the top of the dough and form into an 8-inch round disk. Cut dough into eight equal wedges, and transfer to the baking sheet. Brush with more buttermilk.

5. Bake for 20 to 25 minutes or until golden brown. Allow to cool completely on a rack before glazing.

6. To make icing, in a bowl whisk together lemon juice and powdered sugar. The consistency should be thick yet pourable.

Yield: 8 scones

Prep time: 15 minutes

Bake time: 25 minutes

Cranberry Orange Scones

While many associate the flavors of cranberry and orange with Christmas, these scones are amazing all year round. Bright and citrusy, these buttery scones are made with dried cranberries and orange zest. Be sure to keep all of your ingredients cold for the best results.

INGREDIENTS

2 cups all-purpose flour

1/2 cup white sugar

1/2 teaspoon kosher salt

2 1/2 teaspoons baking powder

zest of 2 oranges

1/2 cup dried cranberries

1/2 cup (1 stick) salted butter, frozen

1/2 cup buttermilk, cold

1 1/2 teaspoons vanilla extract

1 large egg

ICING

2 to 3 tablespoons fresh orange juice

1 cup powdered sugar

DIRECTIONS

1. Preheat oven to 400 degrees. Line a baking sheet with parchment paper.

2. In a bowl whisk together flour, sugar, salt, baking powder, orange zest, and cranberries. Grate frozen butter into flour mixture, toss, and set aside.

3. In a separate bowl whisk together buttermilk, vanilla, and egg. Add to the flour mixture and stir just until it comes together. Do not overmix.

4. Pour dough onto a floured work surface. Flour the top of the dough, and form into an 8-inch round disk. Cut dough into eight equal wedges, and transfer to the baking sheet. Brush with more buttermilk.

5. Bake for 20 to 25 minutes or until golden brown. Allow to cool completely on a rack before glazing.

6. To make icing, in a bowl whisk together orange juice and powdered sugar. The consistency should be thick yet pourable.

Yield: 8 scones

Prep time: 15 minutes

Bake time: 25 minutes

Buttermilk Biscuits

It seems everyone's grandmother has the most perfect buttermilk biscuit recipe. Achieving buttery, flaky pillows of deliciousness is as much about the technique as it is about the ingredients. The key to a great biscuit is frozen grated butter and not overworking the dough. Stirring in the buttermilk just until everything comes together will ensure the dough is not overworked. Folding the dough a couple times will increase the amount of flaky layers in each biscuit. And using a mixture of fats helps prevent the biscuits from becoming dry and allows them to be reheated.

INGREDIENTS

3 ³/₄ cups all-purpose flour

2 tablespoons white sugar

4 teaspoons baking powder

1 teaspoon baking soda

1 teaspoon kosher salt

¹/₄ cup shortening

1 cup (2 sticks) butter, frozen and grated

1 ¹/₂ cups whole buttermilk, cold

Yield: approximately 12 biscuits

Prep time: 15 minutes

Bake time: 15 minutes

DIRECTIONS

1. Preheat oven to 425 degrees.

2. In a large bowl mix together flour, sugar, baking soda, baking powder, and salt.

3. Add shortening. Using a pastry cutter, break up shortening until dough resembles pea-size pieces. Add grated, frozen butter, and toss together in the flour mixture.

4. Add cold buttermilk and stir together until just combined. Do not overmix.

5. Pour out dough onto a floured surface, and sprinkle with a bit more flour. Pat into a rectangle about 1 inch thick. Fold dough into thirds, and pat to 1-inch thickness again. Cut into squares or use a biscuit cutter to make circular biscuits.

6. Place biscuits close together on a baking sheet or in a large cast-iron skillet. Brush tops with buttermilk and bake for 15 minutes. Serve biscuits warm with butter and honey.

Thriftiness Begins with a Shovel and a Teaspoon

Watching Grampa meticulously fold plastic grocery bags and straighten twist ties at the kitchen table seemed funny to me as a kid. Gramma and Grampa saved everything, including space. Clean aluminum foil was folded and stacked next to new rolls. Fabric scraps were saved for patches and braided rugs. Laundry was hung outside on sunny days instead of running the dryer. They were "green" before going green was a thing.

"Throw away in a teaspoon what you bring home in a shovel," Gramma would say. Words to live by.

Both of my grandparents lived very frugally. Both were the youngest of four children, and they themselves have four daughters. Gramma made all of their clothes until they were sixteen, everyone wore hand-me-downs, and everything was mended until it was beyond repair. Even after clothes were no longer wearable, they were still repurposed as rags, doll clothes, or saved for Gramma's quilts.

Stretching a dollar also went into using up every last bit of food. Yesterday's meatloaf became today's sloppy joes, roast chicken became soup, and stale bread was always used as breadcrumbs, French toast, or stuffing for Thanksgiving turkey. Nothing ever went to waste and resourcefulness was next to godliness. Those skills were passed down to their daughters, and then down to the grandkids. Save when times are plentiful, so you'll have enough when times are lean.

In times like a recession, personal financial hardship, or even just because being thrifty is a way of life, learning new ways to minimize food waste is indeed economical. It can also be a new way to exercise your culinary creativity. Here are a few ways to make meals and money stretch.

1. Bananas can be a fickle fruit. Sometimes we buy a few and they're eaten the same day. Other times they sit there uneaten until they go bad. Whether you're planning on putting them in a smoothie or adding them to banana bread, freezing the bananas peeled, cut up, and labeled with the quantity each bag contains will make it easier to use the bananas later. In the case of banana bread, I take the bananas out about an hour or so before I intend to bake with them. Before the bananas are thawed completely, I smash them while they're still a bit cold and proceed with making bread. If you wait too long, the bananas tend to get watery and may ruin the consistency of the bread. Just remember the bread will take a few minutes longer to bake with cold bananas.

2. Leftover veggies and meats can be used in frittatas, stratas, mixed in with scrambled eggs the following morning, or added to soups. In the case of some of the recipes in this book, the same rules apply. Even if you don't have a correct vegetable or fruit, you can always use up what you have.

3. Dairy ingredients like milk, buttermilk, sour cream, and yogurt can still be baked with, up to a week or so after the expiration date. In fact, some of my great-grandmother's recipes call for actual sour milk.

4. Cheese can be salvaged by cutting off the molded part and using the good part. I always store my blocks of cheese wrapped tightly in plastic wrap to cut off the air circulation. I find it slows the molding process, allowing me to take a little longer to use it.

5. Recipes for French toast, bread pudding, strata, brown betty, and strawberry shortcake all originated from stale bread or biscuits. If you've made bread from this book and they're starting to dry out a bit, make sure to transform it into one of the aforementioned recipes to use it up before it's too far gone. You can also cut it into cubes and freeze it for future breadcrumbs, croutons, or stuffing.

6. Jam cake originated from the need to use up extra bits of preserves. You can also substitute different jams in the Strawberry Buttercream Frosting recipe to create different flavors. I like using any sort of berry jam or preserves for this.

7. Store unused nuts in the freezer to keep them fresher longer. They tend to stale in the pantry.

8. At the bakery, we always label and rotate our ingredients, keeping the ones with the closest expiration date in the front. Labeling yours in large print with a Sharpie will help you easily know how long you have to use something. There is also a strict rule that a new package cannot be opened before the old one is used first. This prevents foods from drying out or going bad before you're able to use them.

9. Buying in bulk can save lots of money, but a twenty-five-pound bag of flour can take up quite a bit of room and seem like quite a commitment. I keep my flour and sugar in five-gallon buckets in my laundry room and keep smaller amounts in my pantry. The key is to use it within a year since flour can stale. Active dry yeast can be kept sealed at room temperature for up to two years, but once opened, it should be refrigerated or frozen for up to six months. If you make bread regularly, buying in bulk will save a lot of money. A two-pound package of Red Star active dry yeast can be purchased for as little as $4.50. At that price, a loaf of bread can cost less than fifty cents made at home.

10. If you're anything like me, you like your cookies to remain soft and chewy. After a day or two, they begin to get a little crunchy. Lining your cookie jar or storage container with tissue paper will help them stay softer for longer.

Strawberry Shortcake on Buttermilk Biscuits

Growing up, I always thought strawberry shortcake meant macerated berries over buttermilk biscuits. No little sponges shaped into cups or leftover angel food cake. It was always biscuits. One of the many things I love about this dessert is how economical it is. Usually, this treat was a way to use leftover biscuits from that morning's breakfast with slightly whipped fresh cream poured over the top. In this recipe, a stiffer fresh whipped cream is used, but if you're old school, just whip the cream ingredients together slightly. It's fantastic that way too.

INGREDIENTS

1 pound strawberries

1/4 cup white sugar

1 teaspoon lemon zest

WHIPPED CREAM

1 pint heavy whipping cream

2 tablespoons powdered sugar

1 teaspoon vanilla extract

Buttermilk Biscuits (page 104)

DIRECTIONS

1. To prepare the strawberries, clean, hull, and quarter them, and place in a large bowl. Sprinkle sugar and lemon zest on top, and toss until evenly coated. Cover bowl with plastic wrap and allow to macerate for at least 1 hour. Give the berries a final stir before serving.

2. To prepare the cream, using either an electric mixer or hand mixer, pour heavy whipping cream, powdered sugar, and vanilla into a bowl. For whipped cream, mix cream on high until stiff peaks form. For soft cream, beat until cream thickens slightly but is still pourable.

3. Serve a scoop of strawberries and a dollop of cream over warm biscuits.

Yield: 8 shortcakes

Prep time: 1 hour

Bacon Jalapeño Cheddar Biscuits

Let's take the buttermilk biscuits to the next level by adding jalapeño, cheddar, and bacon, which makes these extra savory, spicy, and all-around delicious. To adjust the heat level, you can add or remove some of the jalapeños, or even add a couple shakes of your favorite hot sauce to really heat things up. Be sure to grate your cheese and chop the jalapeños superfine so they don't impede forming.

INGREDIENTS

3 ³/₄ cups all-purpose flour

2 tablespoons white sugar

1 teaspoon baking soda

4 teaspoons baking powder

1 teaspoon kosher salt

2 tablespoons jalapeños, finely chopped, plus extra jalapeño rounds for garnish

¹/₂ cup shredded sharp Cheddar cheese

3 slices cooked bacon, finely chopped

¹/₄ cup shortening

1 cup (1 stick) butter, frozen and grated

1 ¹/₂ cups buttermilk, cold

Yield: approximately 12 large biscuits

Prep time: 15 minutes

Bake time: 15 minutes

DIRECTIONS

1. Preheat oven to 425 degrees.

2. In a large bowl mix together flour, sugar, baking soda, baking powder, salt, jalapeños, Cheddar, and bacon.

3. Add shortening. Using a pastry cutter, break up shortening until the dough resembles pea-size pieces. Add grated, frozen butter, and toss together in the flour mixture. Add cold buttermilk and stir together until just combined. Do not overmix.

4. Pour out dough onto a floured surface, and sprinkle with a bit more flour. Pat into a rectangle about 1 inch thick. Fold dough into thirds, and pat to 1-inch thickness again. Cut into squares or use a biscuit cutter to make circular biscuits.

5. Place biscuits close together on a baking sheet or in a large cast-iron skillet. Brush tops with buttermilk , add jalapeño rounds, and bake for 15 minutes. Serve biscuits warm with butter and honey.

Happy Eggs

Standing at only five feet tall in her size-six heels, Grandmama Carol was a giant. As the tour director at Crystal Cathedral in Garden Grove, California, when Grandmama gave an order, tour guides who towered over her would hop-to. She was a force to be reckoned with and ran a very tight ship.

Grandmama loved routine at home as much as she did at work. Every weekend we'd visit, and the schedule was always the same: on Saturdays, a construction paper craft, and then off to the mall with the giant merry-go-round before indulging in two pieces of chocolate from her favorite shop. Scrambled eggs and buttered toast with jam before Sunday school. Despite the comfortable predictability of doing the same things, she always made it a fun and memorable adventure.

As she grew older, she became less and less mobile. We began to walk slower so she could keep up, took over driving duty, and carried her purse for her. And then one visit, the routine was over. As young adults, we brought the chocolate to her. We sat and listened to stories about her life: running everywhere instead of walking, playing with her six sisters, splitting a chocolate bar seven ways during the Great Depression, and tending to her grandmother who spoke only German. Her favorite story to tell was when she

and her sister, Eunice, moved to Chicago and went dancing with servicemen on leave and how they liked her especially because she was so petite.

As time passed, arthritis was winning its battle with her, and eventually she needed full-time assistance. But shortly before that, I visited her three times weekly to do chores and keep her company. She was such an extrovert, and I couldn't imagine the loneliness she must have felt being by herself during the days I didn't come.

Back at her apartment, she rested in her blue-and-pink floral rocker while I put away her groceries. I made everything easier to open by cracking lids, breaking the seals on her jam jars, and loosening water bottle tops. I prepped meals and hard-boiled eggs. How a woman who had shrunk well below five feet tall could eat so many eggs in a week, I'll never know, but by God, she had to have her eggs.

As I worked, she told stories about baking pies with her mother-in-law, all the ways her sons got into trouble when they were kids, and the road trips they took across the country every summer. It hurt my heart to hear the wistfulness in her frail little voice. If only her body would cooperate long enough to have an adventure to somewhere other than to the podiatrist or chiropractor. Or heck, if only she had the ability to boil her own eggs. Most of what I prepared was in an effort for her to keep her dignity and freedom for as long as she could manage. The humility of ever-increasing helplessness felt harrowing.

Each visit I brought a surprise with me. After all the years she had made things fun and memorable for my brother and me, I wanted her to have special things too. Sometimes it was a note by her bed or hearts on her bathroom mirror. Other times it was a lap blanket or new music I thought she'd like.

One day I decided to do something unexpected—a way to make her meals less lonely. After we'd returned from a longer day of errands, she collapsed into her rocker and settled into a nap that lasted the remainder of my stay. I was sad to miss out on stories, but it gave me the perfect opportunity to set up her surprise without getting caught. With the egg timer steadily counting down and the last of the meals labeled and put away, I plugged in my glue gun and waited for it to heat up.

With the deed done, a happy note left on her side table, and a stealthy exit, I drove home wondering how long it would take her to notice my little surprise. My phone rang shortly after I'd sat down to dinner, bits of felt and glue still stuck to my fingers. Evidence of mischief.

"Hello? Grandmama, is that you?" I answered, poorly disguising my anticipation.

"My eggs are smiling at me, Sarah!" She laughed into the phone. "What on earth gave you the idea to make tiny people out of my breakfast?" Her unmistakable high-pitched giggle filled my heart. Something as silly as googly eyes glued to eggs had been enough for her to forget her troubles for just a little while. As simple as it was, it was such a welcome bit of cheer.

"Just to keep you company and make you smile until I come back," I replied. "I love you, Grandmama."

Asparagus, Pancetta, and Gouda Strata

Savory bread pudding takes its most delicious form in the strata.
Onions and garlic caramelized in white wine, sautéed asparagus, and
pancetta make this dish exciting and flavorful. Put this dish together
the night before and wake and bake. Future you will thank you.

INGREDIENTS

2 tablespoons butter

1 medium onion, sliced

3 large cloves garlic, minced

1/4 cup dry white wine

kosher salt

3 sprigs fresh thyme

1 bunch asparagus, ends trimmed
and cut into 1-inch pieces

fresh cracked black pepper

12 large eggs

3 cups whole milk

1 1/2 cups shredded aged white
Cheddar

1 1/2 cups shredded Gouda

8 cups brioche or other soft
bread, cubed

4 ounces pancetta, finely sliced

Yield: 12 to 14 servings

Prep time: 30 minutes

Inactive time: 8 hours

Bake time: 1 hour 20 minutes

DIRECTIONS

1. In a large skillet melt the butter and cook the
onions on medium-low until translucent.
Adjust heat to low, add garlic, wine, and a pinch
of salt. Allow mixture to cook down until
onions are caramelized. Add thyme leaves and
asparagus. Cook until asparagus is bright green,
approximately 3 to 5 minutes. Add salt and
pepper to taste. Remove from heat and set aside
to cool for 10 minutes.

2. In a large bowl whisk together eggs and milk.
Add 1 cup each of the Cheddar and Gouda. Fold in
the bread, making sure it's fully coated. Add the
asparagus mix and pancetta, and stir until fully
combined.

3. Pour mixture into a greased 9 x 13-inch pan, and
sprinkle remaining cheese on top. Wrap tightly in
plastic wrap, and refrigerate overnight, or for at
least 8 hours.

4. Preheat oven to 350 degrees. Remove plastic
wrap, cover top with foil, and bake for 30
minutes. Remove foil, and bake for an additional
40 to 50 minutes, or until top is nicely browned
and egg is cooked through.

5. Allow to cool for 10 minutes before serving.

Gruyere-Crusted Savory French Toast with Tomatoes

One of life's greatest pleasures is breakfast for dinner. Whether it's waffles, eggs and bacon, frittata, or French toast, there's something about that comfort food that hits the spot. Most of the time, I gravitate toward savory flavors, and really anytime I can find an excuse to eat more cheese, I jump on it. Usually when people think of French toast, they think of sweet toast topped with maple syrup. Taking a similar concept, I removed all the sugar and spice and replaced it with cheese, garlic, and heat.

INGREDIENTS

1 1/2 cups half-and-half (or whole milk)

3 large eggs

1/2 cup freshly grated Gruyere or Parmesan cheese, divided

2 garlic cloves, grated with microplane or minced extremely fine

1/4 teaspoon salt

1/4 teaspoon fresh cracked black pepper

pinch red pepper flakes

few shakes of hot sauce

6 to 8 slices of rustic bread

butter

olive or canola oil

grape tomatoes, halved

1 clove garlic, minced

fresh basil, sliced thin

DIRECTIONS

1. Set your oven to the warming setting or preheat to 200 degrees and then turn off. You're going to want a warm oven to keep your toasts warm as you finish them.

2. In a bowl whisk together half-and-half, eggs, 1/4 cup Gruyere (or other cheese), garlic, salt, black pepper, red pepper flakes, and hot sauce. Pour the mixture into a wide, shallow dish so it's easier to soak your bread.

3. In a large skillet over medium heat, melt 2 tablespoons of butter and a small splash of olive oil or canola oil. The oil will bring down the smoke point of the butter.

4. Depending on the size of your skillet, cook two to three pieces of bread at a time until each side is golden brown. Move finished pieces to a plate kept in your warm oven while you cook the rest, adding more butter and oil as necessary.

RECIPE CONTINUES

Yield: 6 to 8 toasts

Prep time: 7 minutes

Cook time: 15 to 20 minutes

Total time: 22 to 27 minutes

5. Once all your toasts are finished and inside the oven, add tomatoes, garlic, and 1 tablespoon of butter to the skillet, and cook until softened and fragrant. You still want tomatoes to hold their shape a bit but be slightly browned on the cut side.

6. Plate the French toast and spoon the tomatoes over top. Add the fresh basil and sprinkle more cheese over the toasts before serving.

Roasted Red Pepper and Leek Frittata

Frittatas are the perfect brunch food. Or breakfast. They are the perfect way to use up leftovers, and the combinations are endless. Here is one of my favorite versions.

INGREDIENTS

1 leek

1 tablespoon butter

1 tablespoon olive oil

1/4 cup onion, diced

kosher salt

fresh cracked black pepper

1/4 cup roasted red peppers, chopped

3 cloves garlic, minced

8 large eggs

1/4 cup whole milk

1/2 cup grated Parmesan cheese, divided

1 small wheel of Brie, sliced

DIRECTIONS

1. Cut leek in half lengthwise, discarding top and roots, clean thoroughly, and slice thinly crosswise to create half-moons.

2. In a 12-inch oven-safe skillet over medium heat, melt butter and olive oil together. Once butter bubbles, add leeks and onions, a pinch of salt and pepper, and cook until translucent. Add peppers and garlic and toss together.

3. In a bowl scramble eggs, then add milk and 1/4 cup Parmesan with a little more salt and pepper, and pour into pan with veggies. Mix together carefully, reduce heat to low, and let sit for a few minutes until eggs are halfway cooked.

4. Sprinkle the rest of the Parmesan over the mixture and arrange Brie on top. Broil in oven on high for 5 minutes, or until eggs are puffed up and cheese is bubbly and browned on top. Wiggle the pan to make sure that the center of eggs is done (it shouldn't wiggle). Set on stove and let cool 10 minutes before cutting. Cut wedges and serve.

Yield: 6 to 8 servings

Prep time: 20 to 25 minutes

Bake time: 5 to 10 minutes

Spanish Tortilla Frittata

Taking inspiration from the Spanish tortilla, this frittata uses Yukon gold potatoes for a super creamy texture. The end result is garlicky and buttery in all the right ways. Top with Brie in a brick pattern and fresh green onions for a gorgeous presentation.

INGREDIENTS

4 Yukon Gold potatoes

1 large, sweet Vidalia onion

1 tablespoon butter

1 tablespoon olive oil

kosher salt

fresh cracked black pepper

3 cloves garlic, minced

8 large eggs

$1/4$ cup milk

1 cup grated Romano cheese, divided

1 wheel of Brie, sliced into thin wedges

green onions, sliced on the bias

Yield: 6 to 8 servings

Prep time: 20 to 25 minutes

Bake time: 5 to 10 minutes

DIRECTIONS

1. Thinly slice potatoes, then peel and thinly slice onion.

2. In a 12-inch oven-safe skillet over medium heat, melt butter and olive oil together. Once butter bubbles, add onions, some salt and pepper, and cook until translucent.

3. Reduce heat to low, and add potatoes, cooking until potatoes have softened. Add garlic and cook for 5 minutes more.

4. In a large bowl whisk eggs, milk, and $1/2$ cup Romano with a little more salt and pepper, and pour into pan with the potatoes. Mix together carefully and let cook for a few minutes until eggs are halfway cooked.

5. Sprinkle the rest of the Romano over the mixture and arrange Brie on top in a brick pattern. Broil in oven on high for 5 minutes, or until eggs are puffed up and cheese is bubbly and browned on top. Wiggle the pan to make sure that the center is done (it shouldn't jiggle).

6. Let cool 10 minutes before cutting. Cut wedges and serve. Garnish with fresh green onions.

Artichoke, Sun-Dried Tomato, and Goat Cheese Frittata

With a quick sauté of artichokes, sun-dried tomatoes, and a bit of garlic, this frittata offers a Mediterranean feel. Melty goat cheese gives a tangy earthiness. This frittata is my go-to for a quick, hearty breakfast when we have vegetarian or gluten-sensitive guests coming for brunch.

INGREDIENTS

1 (14-ounce) can quartered artichoke hearts

2 tablespoons butter, melted

2 tablespoons olive oil

kosher salt

fresh cracked black pepper

red pepper flakes

2 tablespoons sun-dried tomatoes in oil, chopped

2 large garlic cloves, peeled and minced

6 to 8 ounces goat cheese, crumbled

10 to 12 leaves basil, cut thinly

8 large eggs

$1/4$ cup whole milk

$1/2$ cup grated Parmesan cheese, divided

Yield: 6 to 8 servings

Prep time: 20 to 25 minutes

Bake time: 5 to 10 minutes

DIRECTIONS

1. Drain and roughly chop artichoke hearts.

2. In a 12-inch oven-safe skillet over medium heat, melt butter and olive oil together. Once butter bubbles, add artichokes, a pinch of salt, pepper, and red pepper flakes, and cook until heated through, approximately 5 minutes.

3. Add tomatoes and garlic, and toss together. Reduce heat to low, and cook for 10 minutes. Crumble goat cheese over top of mixture, cover, and let melt. Stir together and add fresh basil.

4. In a bowl whisk together eggs, milk, and $1/4$ cup Parmesan with a little more salt and pepper, and pour into pan with tomato mixture. Combine together carefully, reduce heat to low, and let sit for a few minutes until eggs are halfway cooked.

5. Sprinkle the rest of the Parmesan on top, and broil in oven on low for 5 to 10 minutes, or until eggs are puffed up and cheese is bubbly and browned on top. Wiggle the pan to make sure that center of eggs is done (it should not jiggle). Let cool 10 minutes before cutting. Cut into wedges and serve.

Sausage, Sage, and Potato Breakfast Casserole

I love a good breakfast casserole. There are hundreds of different options, but nothing says nostalgia quite like a classic sage-y breakfast sausage and potatoes with cheddar. Golden potatoes add the perfect creamy texture, and a generous amount of fresh cracked pepper adds a nice punch.

INGREDIENTS

1 pound breakfast sausage (mild or hot)

1 tablespoon olive oil

1 medium onion, chopped fine

kosher salt

2 to 3 garlic cloves, minced

1 tablespoon fresh sage, minced

4 cups golden potatoes, diced small (1/4 inch)

2–3 tablespoons Anaheim or poblano pepper, diced

fresh ground black pepper

6 large eggs

1/2 cup whole milk

1 cup shredded sharp Cheddar cheese

1 cup shredded aged white Cheddar cheese

DIRECTIONS

1. Preheat oven to 350 degrees. In a large skillet over high heat, cook the sausage in a tablespoon of olive oil until brown and meat is cooked all the way through. Using a slotted spoon, remove sausage from the skillet. Pour out sausage fat, reserving 2 tablespoons in the pan. Turn heat to medium low and cook the onions until translucent.

2. Add garlic, sage, potatoes, and Anaheim or poblano peppers. Season with a pinch of salt and pepper. Cook, stirring occasionally for 10 minutes.

3. In a separate bowl whisk together eggs and milk. Add both cheeses, reserving 1/4 cup of each, and stir to combine.

4. Pour the egg mixture into the sausage and potatoes, and stir to combine. Remove from heat.

5. Pour into a greased 9 x 13-inch casserole dish, and top with the rest of the cheese.

RECIPE CONTINUES

Yield: 8 to 10 servings

Prep time: 15 minutes

Bake time: 30 to 45 minutes

6. Cover with foil and bake for 30 minutes. Then uncover, and bake for an additional 10 minutes, or until potatoes are fully cooked. If you would like your cheese a little browner on top, you can broil on high until desired toastiness is achieved. Allow to cool for 10 minutes before serving.

7. Serve with sliced green onions or avocado and hot sauce.

Cakes and Frostings

Cakes

What's a proper celebration without a cake? Birthdays, weddings, anniversaries—some of our greatest traditions are best celebrated by favorite family recipes or something extra special from the local bakery. To me, nothing is more delightful than a beautifully presented scrumptious homemade cake. Some of my fondest memories were served alongside a slice of these favorites.

Marshmallow Fights

Camping in the Mojave Desert was one of our all-time favorite family activities. My dad's cousin Gary practically lived out there, hauling his family and off-road toys with him for weeks at a time. It's where my mother amazed everyone when she cooked our Thanksgiving turkey in a cardboard box and where we hauled our crispy Christmas tree every year to contribute to the nightly bonfires.

If we were lucky, our caravan of campers would score the largest site shaded by a canopy of pinyon pines. It was the penthouse of campsites and every holiday there was a rush to see who that week's winner would be. Cousin Gary would go out a few days early and hover so he could lay claim and call in the troops. As each motorhome and trailer arrived, they were lined up around the perimeter, creating walls around our dusty fortress. As camp was set up and AstroTurf rolled out, everyone set up their chairs around the giant fire pit—the gathering place.

Every evening after long days of trekking through the desert, as the sun set over the mountain and constellations began to appear in the indigo sky, the bonfire would be lit. Each family would emerge bundled in warm coats from their camper and find a chair by the flames. We'd recount the day's fun, exaggerating stories about all the sweet jumps we'd conquered on our ATVs. Miraculously the hills would get higher and higher with each telling.

As the night went on and the pile of firewood shrunk, Cousin Gary, with wavy gray hair poking out from under his ever-present red polka-dot cap and cigar clenched between his teeth, would quietly sneak away from the fire. As soon as we noticed he'd disappeared, he'd be back donning a mischievous toothy grin and his old aviator goggles on his head. Then, when he was sure he could get away with it, he'd pull a single marshmallow from out of his pocket, wind up, and aim at one of us kids. We'd throw it back and he'd unleash a marshmallow fury and we'd all run to our campers for our own fluffy ammunition and goggles. When we emerged, armed and ready, we found ourselves in the middle of a sugary war zone. The kids versus the adults. They had better aim, but there were more of us. Soon, as the marshmallows were almost indistinguishable from the rocks, we'd find ourselves back at the fire, out of breath and giggling. New, pristine bags of mallows appeared and the fire had died down enough for s'mores.

Whether you start with a battle or simply bring along the proper accoutrements, s'mores are usually something you enjoy together. They're synonymous with campfires and scout songs, counting stars and storytelling. Sure, I've broken out the blowtorch and made one to satisfy a rogue craving, but typically, s'mores are enjoyed among friends and loved ones. They're a fellowship food. At the end of every campfire, the fragrance of smoke clings to us, lingering in our hair and on our clothes—a reminder of the night's conversation and camaraderie.

Sure, I've broken out the blowtorch and made one to satisfy a rogue craving, but typically, s'mores are enjoyed among friends and loved ones.

Cake is also a fellowship food. If you were to ask me what my favorite cake is, without hesitation, I will always answer with an extra-fudgy chocolate cake with brown sugar seven-minute frosting. I love the crystalized layer that forms on the outside of the airy sugar after the cake has been frosted. I love the marriage between the marshmallow toastiness and the intensity of the cocoa sponge. As a little girl, I always asked for this—and only this—to be my birthday cake. There was no other acceptable option.

Over the years I've found that I really enjoy this particular frosting toasted on the outside like one would do with marshmallow. Then I found smoked sea salt. It completed the union between my favorite cake and s'mores. The salty sea air and firewood burning. Edible nostalgia.

When making this cake, take into consideration that the frosting is best the day it's made. You wouldn't make a s'more and save it for later. Likewise, this cake is best enjoyed soon after it's assembled. I typically make the cake a day or two before, wrapping it well to keep it moist, and then make the frosting on the day I intend to serve it. Toasting the frosting with a torch adds an extra layer of smokiness, however it isn't necessary to enjoy the magic.

Campfire Cake

An ode to s'mores, this cake is chocolatey, fudgy, and absolutely amazing with smoky seven-minute frosting. The bonus? You get to toast this frosting with a kitchen torch. Is it optional? Yes. Is it better toasty? Also yes. Will it taste just as good without playing with fire? It will still be delicious. One thing to keep in mind is this frosting is usually best served on the day it's made. This recipe will make three 6-inch round pans, two 8-to 9-inch round pans, or one 9 x 13-inch pan.

INGREDIENTS

2 teaspoons instant coffee

1/2 cup hot water

1 3/4 cups brown sugar

2 cups all-purpose flour

3/4 cup cocoa powder

1 1/2 teaspoons baking soda

2 teaspoons baking powder

1 teaspoon kosher salt

3 large eggs

1 cup buttermilk

1 tablespoon vanilla extract

3/4 cup canola or vegetable oil

crushed graham crackers for garnish

Yield: 1 cake

Prep time: 15 minutes

Bake time: 30 minutes

DIRECTIONS

1. Dissolve the instant coffee in the hot water, and refrigerate for 10 minutes to bring it to room temperature.

2. Preheat oven to 350 degrees. Grease and line pans with parchment paper.

3. In a large bowl combine brown sugar, flour, cocoa, baking soda, baking powder, and salt.

4. In another bowl whisk together eggs, buttermilk, vanilla, and oil.

5. Pour egg mixture into flour mixture, and mix together until there are no lumps. Pour in coffee, and stir together until smooth. Your batter will be loose.

6. Pour into pans in equal amounts, and bake for 25 to 30 minutes, or until toothpick inserted comes out clean.

7. Allow to cool completely on a wire rack before frosting.

8. Frost completely cool cake. If desired, toast frosting with a kitchen torch once cake is decorated. Add graham cracker crumbs to garnish.

Dinner with Maurice

Three of our homes could fit inside of this room," Maurice said as we finished dinner. Sitting in one of the twelve tufted yellow chairs at my meticulously polished antique cherry dining table, I suddenly felt foolish for my attitude. Conviction took a seat at the head of the table, and I shrunk in its shadow.

Earlier that day, our friends, the Ortons, had brought Maurice Odhiambo into my bakery for a cinnamon roll. Before he sat down, he added his dot to our old-school map as every customer had before him. By this time, we'd had a visitor from every state, and at least one from every continent except Antarctica. So when he lifted the US map to access the world map underneath, we were instantly curious about where his dot would land. Kenya.

As he spoke about his ministry, Corey and I exchanged a knowing glance that could mean only one thing: that night we would all break bread over dinner. It had become tradition to invite some of our bakery guests to our home and carry out our own personal mission and ministry of loving people in our community, investing in them as they had invested in us. As usual on nights like these, I left work early to go to the store, gather ingredients, head home, clean the house, and prepare the table.

Wanting to make the evening extra special, I'd carefully planned a veritable feast: hors d'oeuvres, boeuf bourguignon, fresh bread, and a spiced apple Bundt cake. Out came the fancy platters, the coordinated dishes, and stemware that was used only on holidays. In typical Sarah fashion, I'd overplanned, overworried, and overorchestrated. Was there anything I'd made that he couldn't eat for either health or religious purposes? Would it all be enough? My anxiety mounted.

My chronic perfectionism had once again reared its ugly head and stolen my joy in the process.

Without realizing, I'd gone full-Martha leading up to their arrival—scrubbing, straightening, dusting, and polishing everything. I hid the messiness of our personal lives in rooms that wouldn't be seen. I'd fluffed and re-fluffed pillows to their maximum plumpness, trying to achieve that lived-in, but not too lived-in, perfection found in magazines. You know, just your everyday effortless, low-key elegance. Whatever that razor-thin line was, I had convinced myself that I needed to walk it like a tightrope *and* get dinner on the table without leaving a single thing out of place.

My chronic perfectionism had once again reared its ugly head and stolen my joy in the process.

Our guests arrived, and I was still busy in the kitchen, adding finishing touches, plating our food, and making sure the bread was toasted exactly right before bringing everything to the table. Corey took over the entertaining and conversation in the plush library so I could hide my grumbles under the crooning of Dean Martin's velvety voice two rooms away. Finally, everything was ready and I could join the party I'd already missed so much of. With my best "I'm totally not stressed right now" smile, I called everyone to the table.

The realization hit me in the face like an entire humble pie.

Once we were seated, I relaxed and caught up on the conversation. We learned how our friends had met Maurice. He shared the story of growing up in extreme poverty and how it was almost impossible to get out of it. He shared his journey from a single-room shack, to his first pair of shoes at sixteen, to founding his own ministry. As Maurice spoke of building homes for abandoned widows, equipping the homeless with skills to earn a living, and feeding children in the slums made of whatever they could find, I realized that all of my fussing, all of my impatience, and all of my striving to execute this flawless evening wasn't necessary. Here was this man who started with literally nothing—not even shoes—and here I was worried about whether my flatware was shiny enough. The realization hit me in the face like an entire humble pie. Then conviction set in. My agonizing over which napkins to use was so insignificant compared to what my eyes had been opened to.

In that moment, I let it all go. I didn't need to be the hostess with the mostest. I didn't need to be Martha; I needed to be Mary. I needed to be fully present, leaning into every word and every lesson—an education I desperately needed and didn't realize until it was right there in front of me. Perspective is funny that way; it catapults you out of your own self-centered thoughts and straight into reality—and humility.

If I had instead focused on the people, the preparation would not have been stressful. I would have found joy in the anticipation of guests. My thoughts would have been filled with gratefulness instead of anxiousness. Even without the self-imposed rules of perfectionism, the evening would have been just as special—perhaps even more so—un-fluffed pillows and all.

Apple Maple Pecan Cake

Even though this recipe boasts the flavors of autumn, this is one of those cakes that you won't want to wait until fall to make. It reminds me of an apple fritter and a maple donut, but in cake form. Adding pecans takes it up a notch. Walnuts are a great substitute if you don't have pecans. Make sure you really butter and flour your Bundt pan, as those apples love to stick.

INGREDIENTS

1 cup Granny Smith apples, peeled and diced

1 1/4 cups white sugar, divided

2 1/2 cups all-purpose flour

1/4 teaspoon baking soda

3/4 teaspoon baking powder

3/4 teaspoon salt

2 teaspoons ground cinnamon

1/2 teaspoon ground cardamom

1/4 teaspoon ground nutmeg

1/2 teaspoon ground allspice

3/4 cup (1 1/2 sticks) butter, softened

1/3 cup dark brown sugar

2 large eggs

1 tablespoon vanilla extract

1 1/4 cups buttermilk

1 cup pecans, chopped, plus more for garnish

Apple Maple Caramel Glaze (page 167)

DIRECTIONS

1. Toss diced apples in 1/4 cup white sugar, and place in a colander. Place the colander in a large bowl, and allow to drain for 1 hour, reserving juice for the glaze.

2. Preheat oven to 350 degrees. Liberally butter and flour a fluted Bundt pan.

3. In a large bowl whisk together flour, baking soda, baking powder, salt, cinnamon, cardamom, nutmeg, and allspice.

4. In the bowl of an electric mixer fitted with the paddle attachment, cream together butter, remaining 1 cup white sugar, and brown sugar. Add eggs one at a time, beating well after each addition.

5. In a small bowl mix vanilla with buttermilk. Alternate adding flour mixture and buttermilk to the mixer, mixing well after each addition.

6. Fold in the drained apples and the pecans by hand until mixed evenly. Spoon the batter into the prepared Bundt pan, and bake for approximately 45 to 50 minutes, or until a toothpick comes out clean.

RECIPE CONTINUES

Yield: 1 bundt cake

Prep time: 10 minutes

Inactive time: 1 hour

Bake time: 45 to 50 minutes

7. Allow cake to cool for 20 to 30 minutes, then turn out of pan onto cooling rack, and allow to cool completely.

8. Make apple maple caramel glaze on page 167. Drizzle glaze over cooled cake and garnish with pecans.

Mexican Chocolate Bundt Cake with Ganache

One of my favorite ways to take chocolate cake to the next level is to add a bit of heat. In this recipe, ancho chili powder adds the right amount of heat, and coffee intensifies the chocolate flavor, giving it more oomph. Of course, if you aren't a fan of spicy foods, you can use less chili powder, or leave it out altogether. It's still an amazingly decadent chocolate cake!

INGREDIENTS

1 pound (4 sticks) butter, softened

2 cups white sugar

6 large eggs

2 teaspoons vanilla extract

1 tablespoon brewed coffee

2 1/2 cups all-purpose flour

1 teaspoon kosher salt

1 teaspoon baking powder

1/2 cup Dutch cocoa powder

1/2 teaspoon ground ancho chili powder (optional)

1/4 cup chopped pistachios

GANACHE

1/2 cup heavy cream

1 cup finely chopped dark chocolate

1 teaspoon vanilla extract

DIRECTIONS

1. Preheat oven to 300 degrees with rack placed in the center position in the oven. Grease a fluted Bundt pan, and coat with cocoa powder.

2. In the bowl of an electric mixer fitted with the paddle attachment, cream together butter and sugar on low until it makes a paste. Then beat on high until light and fluffy, approximately 5 minutes. Scrape down sides of the bowl occasionally, making sure the texture is consistent throughout.

3. Add eggs one at a time, beating well after each addition. Add vanilla and coffee, and combine.

4. In a separate bowl sift together flour, salt, baking powder, cocoa, and ancho chili powder. Add to egg mixture, and combine just until flour is completely mixed in. Scoop batter into prepared Bundt pan, and spread evenly with a spatula.

5. Bake for 1 hour and 20 minutes, or until a toothpick comes out clean. Allow to cool for 1 hour, then remove from Bundt pan, and allow to cool completely.

RECIPE CONTINUES

Yield: 1 bundt cake

Prep time: 10 minutes

Bake time: 1 hour 20 minutes

6. To make ganache, microwave the heavy cream until almost boiling. Pour over chocolate chips, and allow to sit for 5 minutes. Then stir together until completely smooth. If chocolate doesn't melt completely, you can microwave it for 10-second increments, until chocolate is completely melted and smooth. Add vanilla and stir until smooth.

7. To assemble, pour ganache evenly over top of the Bundt cake and allow to drip down. Sprinkle with chopped pistachio nuts.

1850s Gingerbread Spice Cake with Mascarpone Buttercream

Of all the recipes found hidden in my great-grandmother's cookbook, this one is the oldest, dating back more than 170 years. It was the first of her recipes that made it into my oven, and when the door opened, Christmas morning danced out in a cloud of nostalgia. It was a molasses cookie in cake form. I created a mascarpone buttercream to add a bit of tart sweetness.

INGREDIENTS

1/2 cup (1 stick) butter, softened

1/2 cup white sugar

1 large egg

1 teaspoon vanilla extract

2 1/2 cups all-purpose flour

1 1/2 teaspoons baking soda

1 teaspoon ground cinnamon

1 teaspoon ground ginger

1/2 teaspoon ground cloves

1/2 teaspoon ground allspice

1 teaspoon kosher salt

1 cup molasses

1 cup buttermilk

Mascarpone Buttercream
  (page160)

Yield: 9 x 9-inch cake

Prep time: 10 minutes

Bake time: 45 minutes

DIRECTIONS

1. Preheat oven to 350 degrees. Line a 9 x 9-inch pan with parchment paper, and grease with nonstick spray.

2. In the bowl of an electric mixer cream together butter and sugar. Beat until light and fluffy, approximately 5 minutes. Add egg and vanilla, and beat until fluffy.

3. In a separate bowl whisk together flour, baking soda, cinnamon, ginger, cloves, allspice, and salt.

4. In another bowl whisk together molasses and buttermilk.

5. Add flour and buttermilk mixture to mixer in three parts, alternating between the two and mixing well after each addition.

6. Pour into prepared pan and smooth top.

7. Bake for 45 minutes, or until a toothpick comes out clean. Allow to cool for 30 minutes in the pan, then move to a cooling rack to cool completely.

8. Prepare the mascarpone buttercream (recipe on page 160), and spread over completely cooled cake.

9. Lightly dust cake with cinnamon or other preferred spice and serve.

Blueberry Peach Cake

When plump, juicy blueberries merge with ripe peaches,
prepare yourself for what tastes like summer decadence.

INGREDIENTS

1 cup diced fresh peaches

1 1/4 cups white sugar, divided

1 cup fresh blueberries

2 1/2 cups plus 2 tablespoons
  all-purpose flour, divided

1/4 teaspoon baking soda

3/4 teaspoon baking powder

3/4 teaspoon kosher salt

3/4 cups (1 1/2 sticks) butter

2 large eggs

1 tablespoon vanilla extract

1 1/4 cups buttermilk

additional fruit for garnish

ICING

reserved peach juice

1 teaspoon vanilla extract

1 cup powdered sugar

Yield: 1 bundt cake

Prep time: 10 minutes

Inactive time: 1 hour

Bake time: 35 to 45 minutes

DIRECTIONS

1. Toss diced peaches in 1/4 cup white sugar, and
   place in a colander. Place colander in a large
   bowl, and allow to drain for 1 hour, reserving
   juice for the icing. Rinse blueberries and toss in
   2 tablespoons of flour to coat.

2. Preheat oven to 350 degrees. Liberally butter and
   flour a fluted Bundt pan.

3. In a large bowl whisk together remaining flour,
   baking soda, baking powder, and salt.

4. In the bowl of an electric mixer fitted with the
   paddle attachment, cream together butter and
   remaining 1 cup white sugar. Add eggs one at a
   time, beating well after each addition.

5. In a separate bowl mix vanilla into buttermilk.
   Alternate adding flour mixture and buttermilk to
   the mixer, mixing well after each addition.

6. Fold in the drained peaches and dredged
   blueberries by hand until mixed evenly. Spoon
   the batter into the prepared Bundt pan, and bake
   for approximately 35 to 45 minutes, or until a
   toothpick comes out clean.

7. Allow cake to cool for 20 to 30 minutes, turn out of
   pan onto cooling rack, and allow to cool completely.

8. To make icing, in a bowl whisk together peach juice,
   vanilla, and powdered sugar. If icing is thin, add
   additional powdered sugar until thick but pourable.

9. Move cake to serving plate or stand, drizzle with
   icing, and garnish with fresh fruit.

The Peach Tree on Primrose Lane

Gramma's garden was always teeming with fruits and vegetables. Neat rows of sweet carrots and cabbage were nestled in the small space next to the house, orange and lemon trees grew in each corner, and along the fence grew a wall of green beans that never seemed to run out. In warmer months, my brother and I would turn the picnic table into a fort with Gramma's collection of 1970s flower blankets, where we would eat peanut butter sandwiches and fresh green beans off the vine as she pruned and harvested. After lunch, she would call us over and show us how to tell if tomatoes and bell peppers were ripe for picking and let us "help" her play in the dirt.

Beyond the cinderblock fence in Gramma and Grampa's backyard grew an enormous peach tree. Its branches stretched far above the one-story ranch houses that lined Primrose Lane. Southern California was so warm year-round, the tree was always dressed in emerald-green leaves, even in winter. It wasn't uncommon for each house in older neighborhoods to have fruit trees and for neighbors to share their abundance.

Every summer when the tree began to bend under the weight of the fruit, Grampa would zip-tie a small picking basket to the end of a pole and hoist it high into the leaves to gather hundreds of giant peaches the size of velvety softballs. As he plucked, he'd lower the basket so we could transfer the sweet fruits into metal buckets and carry them into the house where Gramma would be waiting. She sorted them into piles for canning, pies, and baskets to share with the neighbors. It seemed the more Grampa picked, the more fruit grew in its place. Even when the buckets were overflowing, the tree was still full after a day's work. All summer long, the tree provided.

The more Grampa picked, the more fruit grew in its place.

"The more we take care of the tree, the more fruit it bears," Grampa explained, turning on the garden hose he left draped over the wall. He regularly watered the tree even though it wasn't in his own yard. I suppose that was his way of thanking the neighbors for letting him pick peaches. "Even if we can't eat it all, it's okay. We can always share with others. But if we stop picking so much, the tree won't make as many peaches next year."

Grampa sure knows a lot about trees, I thought, taking a big bite out of a peach. At eight years old, I thought it was funny that a tree would want to make more fruit when you picked it. It seemed like the tree would become discouraged from growing more because of all the hard work it had put into the fruit it already made.

It wouldn't make sense until a while later when Gramma took me around to the other side. The neighbors who owned the tree never picked fruit on their side, so they didn't have much fruit at all. The tree had grown so large, they couldn't see the side that hung over into my grandparents' backyard. Even on the same tree, which shared the same roots, the side that was picked from produced more fruit than the side that was left alone. In fact, Gramma regularly gave buckets of peaches and jam to the neighbors who owned the tree!

Looking back at that tree now, I see that the peaches were a metaphor for a lesson that Gramma and Grampa were trying to teach us. The gifts that we have in life can grow depending on how much we work on them. If we nurture them regularly and carefully, we'll have abundance for ourselves, and plenty to share with others. Our gifts are not meant to be kept to ourselves. They are meant to be shared with others.

Gifts and relationships flourish because of the work we put into growing them. Those gifts that aren't nurtured won't grow, even when they're connected to other gifts that are tended to regularly, like the tree that grows fruit on only one side.

Peach Bourbon Upside-Down Cake

One of my favorite summer treats is a peach upside-down cake. It's similar to pineapple, except it takes advantage of peaches during their peak season. The splash of bourbon adds complex flavor that complements the peaches. It's best to use peaches that are slightly underripe, so they hold their shape during baking. Overripe peaches tend to break down a little too much, leaving you with a mushy texture. If you want to make pineapple upside-down cake instead, simply substitute fresh pineapple and maraschino cherries.

FRUIT FILLING

2 tablespoons butter, melted

1/2 cup dark brown sugar

3 peaches, sliced 1/3 inch thick

2 tablespoons lemon juice, fresh squeezed

1 teaspoon good bourbon

BATTER

2 large eggs

1 cup white sugar

1 teaspoon vanilla extract

1 teaspoon good bourbon

1 cup all-purpose flour

1/4 teaspoon salt

1 1/2 teaspoons baking powder

2 tablespoons butter, melted

1/2 cup buttermilk

DIRECTIONS

1. Preheat oven to 350 degrees and place an oven rack in the middle of the oven.

2. Mix together the 2 tablespoons of melted butter and dark brown sugar. Sprinkle in a 9-inch round pan. Toss together the sliced peaches, lemon juice, and bourbon. Arrange the peaches in concentric circles on top of the brown sugar.

3. In the bowl of an electric mixer fitted with the paddle attachment, beat the eggs on high until thick and fluffy. Slowly add the sugar. Add the vanilla and bourbon and beat again.

4. In a separate bowl whisk together flour, salt, and baking powder.

5. In a saucepan heat the butter and buttermilk until steaming but not boiling. Alternately add flour mixture and buttermilk mixture to the mixer. Once batter is completely combined (it will be thin), pour over peaches.

RECIPE CONTINUES

Yield: One 9-inch cake

Prep time: 15 minutes

Bake time: 40 minutes

6. Bake for 40 minutes, or until a toothpick inserted comes out clean. Allow to cool for 10 minutes. Run a knife between the cake and the pan to loosen. Then invert onto your serving plate. Carefully lift the pan straight up. Serve warm with vanilla ice cream.

Evil Eva's Plain Cake

Here it is! My great-grandmother's plain cake recipe. Some slight changes, translations, or guesses had to be made in order to bake properly. The only instructions on the original recipe are "Mix as given," so I don't feel too terrible making some changes. Both the Rocky Road Frosting and the Strawberry Jam Buttercream are fantastic on this!

INGREDIENTS

1/3 cup butter or shortening

1 cup white sugar

3 large eggs

2 teaspoons vanilla extract

2 cups all-purpose flour

1 tablespoon baking powder

1/4 teaspoon salt

2/3 cup whole milk

DIRECTIONS

1. Preheat oven to 350 degrees, placing a rack in the center of the oven. Prepare two 9-inch round pans by lining the bottoms with parchment and spraying with nonstick spray.

2. In the bowl of an electric mixer fitted with the paddle attachment, cream together butter and sugar until light and fluffy, approximately 5 minutes. Beat in eggs one at a time, scraping down sides. Add vanilla and mix well.

3. In a separate bowl sift together flour, baking powder, and salt. Add to the mixer, alternating with milk, mixing well after each addition.

4. Pour into prepared pans, and bake for 22 to 25 minutes, or until a toothpick comes out clean. Remove from oven, and let cool for 30 minutes before removing from pan. Set on rack to cool completely before frosting.

Yield: One 2-layer cake

Prep time: 10 minutes

Bake time: 22 to 25 minutes

Flourless Chocolate Cake

A chocolate cake so decadent, you'd never believe it was gluten-free. Actually, it's right in the name—flourless—but still. Even if you don't have dietary restrictions, this is an absolutely amazing cake. Because it's so incredibly rich, you'll want to serve thin slices. The upside is you're able to serve more people!

INGREDIENTS

½ cup (1 stick) salted butter

1 cup semisweet chocolate chips

¼ teaspoon kosher salt

1 cup white sugar

2 teaspoons vanilla extract

2 teaspoons brewed coffee

3 large eggs

½ cup high-quality cocoa powder

Ganache (page 171)

Yield: 12 to 14 servings

Prep time: 30 minutes

Inactive time: 3 hours

Cook time: 25 to 28 minutes

DIRECTIONS

1. Line an 8-inch round cake pan with parchment and coat with nonstick cooking spray.

2. In a double boiler, or heatproof bowl over a saucepan with a couple inches of simmering water, melt the butter and chocolate chips until smooth. Remove from heat and allow to cool for 5 minutes.

3. Whisk in salt, sugar, vanilla, and coffee. Whisk eggs into batter until well-combined. Whisk in cocoa powder until completely smooth. Pour batter into prepared cake pan and spread evenly.

4. Bake for 25 to 28 minutes, or until a toothpick comes out clean. Allow to cool for 10 minutes. Then invert cake onto a cooling rack and immediately turn right side up onto another cooling rack. Cool completely.

5. Make the ganache using the recipe on page 171. Pour over the cake and spread with an offset spatula. Allow to set for 3 to 4 hours before serving. Serve with ice cream or fruit. Or both.

Carol's Carrot Cake

This ultra-dense, ultra-moist, ultra-carroty cake is everything I imagine when I think of carrot cake. Mixing both brown and white sugars together gives this cake an added hint of warmth and extra deliciousness.

INGREDIENTS

4 cups all-purpose flour

2 tablespoons ground cinnamon

2 teaspoons ground nutmeg

2 teaspoons baking soda

1/2 teaspoon baking powder

2 teaspoons kosher salt

1 1/2 cups canola oil

2 cups white sugar

1 cup dark brown sugar

6 large eggs

4 cups grated carrots

4 teaspoons vanilla extract

1 cup chopped walnuts or pecans, plus extra for garnish

Cream Cheese Frosting (page 159)

Yield: One 9x13 cake

Prep time: 20 minutes

Bake time: 1 hour 15 minutes

DIRECTIONS

1. Preheat oven to 325 degrees.

2. In a large bowl whisk together flour, cinnamon, nutmeg, baking soda, baking powder, and salt.

3. In the bowl of an electric mixer fitted with the paddle attachment, cream together canola oil, white sugar, and brown sugar. Beat in eggs, one at a time, until light and fluffy. Add the grated carrot and vanilla, and combine. Add flour mixture and combine just until it comes together. Fold in 1 cup walnuts.

4. Pour batter into a greased 9 x 13-inch baking dish.

5. Bake for 1 hour and 15 minutes, or until a toothpick inserted in the middle comes out clean. Cool cake completely.

6. Make cream cheese frosting on page 159 and cover cake. Garnish with more nuts.

7. To make muffins, line muffin tins with liners, and fill about 3/4 of the way full. Bake for 30 to 35 minutes, or until a toothpick comes out clean. Remove from muffin tins to cool and enjoy, or make it a cupcake by adding frosting.

Orange Pound Cake

Buttery and bright citrus notes make this cake a year-round treat. Valencia oranges are my favorite for baking since they tend to have the brightest, sweetest flavor. However, navel and other varieties will make a delicious cake too.

INGREDIENTS

1 pound (4 sticks) salted butter, softened

2 cups white sugar

6 large eggs

2 teaspoons vanilla extract

zest from 2 oranges

3 cups all-purpose flour

1 teaspoon kosher salt

1 teaspoon baking powder

GLAZE

juice of 1 orange

1 cup powdered sugar

1 teaspoon vanilla extract

DIRECTIONS

1. Preheat oven to 300 degrees and place a rack in the center position in the oven. Grease a fluted Bundt pan and coat with flour.

2. In the bowl of an electric mixer fitted with the paddle attachment, cream together butter and sugar on low until it makes a paste. Then beat on high until light and fluffy, approximately 5 minutes. Scrape down sides of the bowl occasionally, making sure the texture is consistent throughout.

3. Add eggs one at a time, beating well after each addition. Add vanilla and orange zest and combine.

4. In a separate bowl sift together flour, salt, and baking powder. Add to flour mixture, and combine just until flour is completely mixed in. Scoop batter into prepared Bundt pan, and spread evenly with a spatula.

5. Bake for 1 hour and 20 minutes, or until a toothpick comes out clean. Allow to cool for 1 hour, then remove from Bundt pan, and allow to cool completely.

RECIPE CONTINUES

Yield: 1 bundt cake

Prep time: 10 minutes

Bake time: 1 hour 20 minutes

6. To make glaze, in a bowl whisk together orange juice with powdered sugar and vanilla. Glaze should be thick but still pourable.

7. Cut away rind from each orange by slicing off each end and then cutting the rind away from the fruit in strips. Once the rind is removed, cut the oranges into thin rounds.

8. To assemble, pour glaze evenly over top of the Bundt cake, and allow to drip down. Decorate with the orange slices and serve.

Berry Brown Betty

Similar to a cobbler, a Brown Betty is fresh or frozen fruit layered with day-old bread. The tartness of the berries mixed with the sweetness of the crisp, buttery brioche is perfection. Top it with a scoop or two of vanilla ice cream, and it becomes pure magic.

INGREDIENTS

3 cups mixed berries

$^1\!/_2$ cup plus 2 tablespoons white sugar, divided

4 tablespoons ($^1\!/_2$ stick) butter, melted and divided

1 tablespoon lemon juice, fresh squeezed

2 teaspoons lemon zest

pinch kosher salt

6 slices brioche, torn into small pieces

DIRECTIONS

1. Preheat oven to 350 degrees. Grease a 10-inch cast-iron skillet with butter.

2. In a bowl toss berries with $^1\!/_2$ cup of sugar, 2 tablespoons of melted butter, lemon juice, zest, and salt.

3. In a separate bowl toss bread in remaining 2 tablespoons of melted butter and remaining 2 tablespoons of sugar.

4. Layer half of the berries in the bottom of the skillet, followed by a layer of bread. Layer the other half of the berries, and top with the remaining bread.

5. Bake covered for 30 minutes. Uncover and bake for an additional 15 to 20 minutes, or until the bread is golden brown. Allow to cool for 10 minutes before serving. Serve alone or with vanilla ice cream.

Yield: One 10-inch skillet

Prep time: 15 minutes

Bake time: 45 to 50 minutes

Smashing Fruit

Balancing on a wooden stool in my grandmother's kitchen on Primrose Lane, I plunged my hands into a sink full of warm tomatoes. That day all four of Gramma's daughters were crowded around the stove, stirring burbling strawberries and sterilizing glass jars with shiny lids. I'd been recruited from watching Saturday-morning cartoons with Grampa to be the tomato smasher.

"How else will you know they've all been crushed evenly?" Gramma asked. "Here, just stick your hands in there, and do like this!"

I watched her pick up a peeled red orb and squeeze. Gripping one, I copied her, crushing it with surprising ease. Feeling the warm, slippery fruits burst in my own hands was horrifying and yet oddly satisfying at the same time. The seeds tickled as they escaped between my fingers. With my sleeves rolled up above my elbows, tied up in a too-big, soft frayed apron, and my long blonde French braids tucked safely out of the way, I dove into the task with eager hands. Why had this never been allowed before now? I giggled mischievously, amused at the thought of squishing all my mother's tomatoes at home. *Boy, would she be mad.*

As my fingers felt around the basin for more and more tomatoes to squash, the assembly line of jam continued behind me. Jars were filled, sealed, and lined up like steamy soldiers on Gramma's dining room table. White cotton flour sack towels had been laid over the top to protect the oak beneath. Bright red, molten strawberries gleamed in the sunlight pouring through the sliding glass door. The air was thick with the sweetness of berries, chatter, and laughter. Each of my aunts had such a distinct laugh that to hear them all together was a chorus of joy. It didn't matter what the four sisters were doing together, whether it was camping, gardening, canning, baking pies, or planned trips to my parents' beach house, that infectious laughter was ever present.

I may have been many years away from canning anything myself, but what I remember most about days like that was the togetherness.

Above the kitchen table, Grampa's brass ship wheel clock chimed happily at the top of the hour. The same little clock had been daintily keeping time for the four Allen girls since they were children. As kids, my brother and I would awaken to its happy song accompanying the fragrance of peaches and whipped cream on waffles, beckoning us to the kitchen for breakfast. Its sound only added to the cheerfulness of that fruit-smashing day.

Soon the task of strawberry jam was complete, and the canning of the tomato slurry I'd created would begin. At eight years old, I was still a little too young to help with much more than smashing fruit, but rather than returning to *Popeye*, I sat at the table. No offense to Olive Oyl and Wimpy, but canning was way more fun than cartoons.

I watched as round two began, and the smell of cooking tomatoes filled the air, merging with the strawberries. As more jars and lids went into the boiling water, the stories continued. The aunts challenged me to count all the pops I heard, signifying the cans had properly sealed. It wasn't long before I'd lost count.

Besides, it was easy to get sidetracked listening to their exciting tales of growing up. My favorite story was hearing about when Aunt Nancy had gotten her long hair trapped in the stand mixer, and Aunt Teena had to turn it off because my mother was too busy laughing to help. I didn't know sisters still acted like sisters to one another when they grew up.

I may have been many years away from canning anything myself, but what I remember most about days like that was the togetherness. Reminiscing about when they were young, stories of childhood and past adventures, inside jokes and tales of funny mishaps. It seemed like whenever all the sisters gathered together with Gramma, love and fun were ever present.

Jam Cake

One of my favorite things about jam cake is that you can have it any time of the year. You don't have to wait for fresh fruit to come into season for berries. It's also a great way to use up all of the last bits of jam in the fridge. Typically, I always have an array of jams when we sit down to family breakfast, so there's always three or four varieties open at any given time. If you're the same way, you can create your own blend, or if you're a purist, you can just use one. Some people like a glaze over the top, but I like mine with fresh whipped cream with a little more jam added in.

INGREDIENTS

1 cup (2 sticks) salted butter, softened

1 cup sugar

3 large eggs

2 teaspoons vanilla extract

1 cup jam of your choice

2 1/2 cups all-purpose flour

1/2 teaspoon kosher salt

1 teaspoon baking soda

1 teaspoon ground nutmeg

1/2 teaspoon ground allspice

Yield: 1 bundt cake

Prep time: 10 minutes

Bake time: 45 to 55 minutes

DIRECTIONS

1. Preheat oven to 350 degrees. Place a rack in the center position of the oven. Grease a fluted Bundt pan with butter, and coat with flour.

2. In the bowl of an electric mixer fitted with the paddle attachment, cream together butter and sugar until it makes a paste. Then beat on high until light and fluffy, approximately 5 minutes. Scrape down the sides of the bowl occasionally, making sure the texture is consistent throughout.

3. Add eggs one at a time, beating after each addition. Add vanilla and combine. Add jam and combine thoroughly.

4. In a separate bowl sift together flour, salt, baking soda, nutmeg, and allspice. Add flour and buttermilk alternately to mixer, and combine until smooth.

5. Bake for 45 to 55 minutes, or until a toothpick inserted into the middle comes out clean. Allow to cool for 1 hour before removing from the pan. Cool completely on a cooling rack.

Frostings, Icings, and Fillings

Some people use frosting and icing interchangeably, but there is a big difference—including ingredients, technique, and texture. Generally speaking, icing is thinner and sometimes glossier while frosting is much thicker and fluffier. Frosting also acts as filling, whereas icing does not. Filling is still its own thing, as some fillings would never be used as frostings. Experiment with some of these favorites and experience the differences for yourself. You just might discover your go-to for topping your favorite cakes and other baked goods.

Cream Cheese Frosting

While cream cheese frosting is fantastic on cakes, it is also magical on cinnamon rolls. When spread on while the rolls are hot, this frosting melts into all the nooks and crannies, making for a truly divine experience. This frosting is also fabulous spread on banana bread and as the filling of the Cream Cheese Rolls (page 81).

INGREDIENTS

10 tablespoons salted butter, softened

1 (8-ounce) package cream cheese, softened

4 cups powdered sugar, sifted

1 tablespoon vanilla extract

DIRECTIONS

1. Cream together butter and cream cheese in the bowl of an electric mixer fitted with the paddle attachment, occasionally scraping down the sides to ensure even mixing.

2. Add powdered sugar 1 cup at a time, mixing on low and then whipping on high.

3. Add vanilla and give a final whip. If frosting is too thick, add a tablespoon of milk. Frosting should be thick like cake frosting.

Yield: makes enough to cover a two-layer cake or 12 cinnamon rolls

Prep time: 5 minutes

Mascarpone Buttercream Frosting

The marriage of tartness and sweetness makes this the perfect frosting for cakes and cupcakes alike. Different from cream cheese frosting, mascarpone buttercream is especially wonderful on the 1850s Gingerbread Spice Cake found on page 137, though it can easily work on many of the cakes found in these pages.

INGREDIENTS

10 tablespoons salted butter, softened

8 ounces mascarpone, softened

4 cups powdered sugar, sifted

1 tablespoon vanilla extract

DIRECTIONS

1. Cream together butter and mascarpone in the bowl of an electric mixer fitted with the paddle attachment, occasionally scraping down the sides to ensure even mixing.

2. Add powdered sugar 1 cup at a time, mixing on low and then whipping on high.

3. Add vanilla and give a final whip. Don't overmix as it will cause the frosting to separate.

Yield: makes enough to cover a two-layer or 9x13 cake

Prep time: 5 minutes

Rocky Road Frosting

If rocky road ice cream was a frosting, this would definitely be it. Drizzling melted chocolate into a glorious buttercream frosting creates a decadent flavor without being too sweet. Since it's one of Great-Grandma Eva's recipes, it seems only fitting to use it to frost Evil Eva's Plain Cake found on page 145. Not so plain anymore!

INGREDIENTS

4 squares bittersweet chocolate, chopped

$1/4$ cup ($1/2$ stick) unsalted butter

$1/2$ cup (1 stick) salted butter, softened

4 cups powdered sugar, sifted

1 teaspoon vanilla extract

4 tablespoons whole milk

$1/8$ teaspoon kosher salt

1 cup mini marshmallows

$1/2$ cup chopped pecans, walnuts, or peanuts

chocolate syrup

DIRECTIONS

1. Melt chocolate and $1/4$ cup unsalted butter in a double boiler until just melted. Remove from heat.

2. In the bowl of an electric mixer fitted with the whisk attachment, cream salted butter. Add powdered sugar 1 cup at a time. Combine and then whip on high after each addition. Add vanilla, combine on low, and then whip on high. Add milk 1 tablespoon at a time, whipping after each addition.

3. Add the melted chocolate mixture, combine, and then whip until light and fluffy. Layer the marshmallows and pecans over the frosting, or between the layers of cake. Drizzle with chocolate syrup.

Yield: 2 cups (enough for 1 sheet cake)

Prep time: 10 minutes

Smoky Seven-Minute Frosting

If asked what my favorite frosting of all time is, I wouldn't let you finish your question before I answered with this one. Whether you make it with smoked salt or kosher salt, it will still taste like marshmallows and happiness. I think it's best covering chocolate cake.

INGREDIENTS

2 egg whites, unbeaten

1 cup white sugar

1/2 cup dark brown sugar

1/2 teaspoon cream of tartar

1/3 cup cold water

1 teaspoon smoked sea salt

2 teaspoons vanilla extract

DIRECTIONS

1. Fill the bottom half of a double boiler with a couple inches of water. Make sure the water does not touch the upper bowl. Heat the water until it's just boiling.

2. Put the egg whites, white sugar, brown sugar, cream of tartar, cold water, and smoked sea salt into the top of a double boiler (not over the heat yet). Using a hand mixer, beat for 1 minute on low to blend.

3. Place top of double boiler over boiling water, and beat constantly on highest setting, for 7 minutes. To prevent overcooking, remove top and continue to beat on high until stiff peaks form.

4. Add vanilla and beat until combined and a spreading consistency is reached. Frosting should be light and glossy.

5. Frost completely cool cake.

Yield: makes enough to cover a 2 layer 9-inch cake

Prep time: 10 minutes

Strawberry Jam Buttercream Frosting

To get the best strawberry jam frosting, you will need the best strawberry jam. Store-bought will work but visiting the farmers' market for homemade jam will really make this one shine.

INGREDIENTS

½ cup (1 stick) butter, softened

2 teaspoons vanilla extract

3 tablespoons whole milk or cream

4 cups powdered sugar, sifted

¼ cup strawberry preserves

DIRECTIONS

1. In the bowl of an electric mixer, beat the butter until light and fluffy. Add the vanilla and milk, and beat until combined.

2. Add the powdered sugar 1 cup at a time, mixing slowly at first, and then beat on high until fully combined and smooth.

3. Add the strawberry preserves, mix on low to combine, and then on high until light and fluffy. If the frosting is too thin, add a bit more powdered sugar until piping consistency is reached.

4. To store, keep in an airtight container in the fridge for up to 3 to 4 days. To use, warm to room temperature.

Yield: makes enough to cover a 2-layer 9-inch cake

Prep time: 10 minutes

Buttermilk Icing

A quick icing for a Bundt cake, cinnamon rolls, or shortbread cookies, this takes a typical drizzle up a notch, making it creamier and slightly tangy. Add dried strawberries or lemon zest for added flavor.

INGREDIENTS

2 cups powdered sugar, sifted

4 to 5 tablespoons buttermilk

2 teaspoons vanilla extract

DIRECTIONS

1. Sift powdered sugar in a bowl.

2. Add buttermilk 2 tablespoons at a time until icing can be drizzled. Add the vanilla extract and stir to combine. Use immediately or refrigerate in a sealed container for up to 1 week. Stir well before use.

Yield: makes enough to drizzle 12 cinnamon rolls or 8 scones

Prep time: 5 minutes

Maple Bourbon Icing

This simple icing is made with real maple syrup and just a splash of bourbon for a little kick. Add a dash of maple extract to give that essence of a donut shop maple bar, and you've got the perfect drizzle for cakes or cinnamon rolls.

INGREDIENTS

2 cups powdered sugar

¼ cup real maple syrup

½ teaspoon bourbon

½ teaspoon vanilla extract

¼ teaspoon maple extract

2 teaspoons water, as needed

DIRECTIONS

1. In a bowl whisk together powdered sugar, maple syrup, bourbon, vanilla, and maple extract.

2. If consistency is too thick to drizzle, add a couple teaspoons of water until drizzling consistency is reached. Use immediately or store refrigerated in a sealed container for up to 1 week. Stir well before use.

Yield: makes enough to drizzle 12 cinnamon rolls

Prep time: 5 minutes

Apple Maple Caramel Glaze

This quick caramel is glorious over the Apple Maple Pecan Cake or even over the Apple Streusel cinnamon rolls. Heck, it's even great over ice cream!

INGREDIENTS

2 tablespoons butter

$^1/_4$ cup apple juice

$^1/_2$ cup pure maple syrup

2 tablespoons heavy cream

1 teaspoon vanilla extract

DIRECTIONS

1. In a saucepan over medium heat, melt butter.

2. Add apple juice, maple syrup, heavy cream, and vanilla.

3. Bring to a boil, and allow to simmer until thickened, approximately 5 to 10 minutes. Allow to cool to room temperature. To serve, pour over Bundt cake.

Yield: makes enough to drizzle 1 bundt cake or 12 cinnamon rolls

Prep time: 20 minutes

Orange Glaze

Orange and caramel-y, this glaze is delicious over the orange bundt cake or even drizzled over cinnamon rolls. Made with dark brown sugar, the molasses gives this glaze a beautiful depth of flavor.

INGREDIENTS

1/2 cup (1 stick) salted butter

1 cup dark brown sugar

1/4 cup orange juice

1 tablespoon orange zest

1/2 teaspoon kosher salt

1/4 cup heavy cream

2 teaspoons vanilla extract

DIRECTIONS

1. In a medium saucepan over medium heat, melt butter and sugar together.

2. Pour in orange juice, orange zest, and salt.

3. Bring to a boil, and slowly stir in cream. Simmer and reduce heat to medium-low once it comes to a gentle boil. Stir until thickened enough to coat the back of a spoon, approximately 4 to 6 minutes.

4. Stir in vanilla. Remove from heat, and cool for at least 10 minutes before pouring over cake.

Yield: Makes enough to cover 1 bundt cake

Prep time: 20 minutes

Cinnamon Filling

Whenever I think of the ultimate cinnamon filling, I think of amazingly fragrant, buttery, caramel-y magic. This five-ingredient filling has all the complexity and magic you'd expect from the perfect cinnamon roll, braided bread, or heck, even on waffles or toast. The key is to make sure you start with room-temperature butter and whip all of the ingredients into a fluffy paste similar to a cake frosting. You want to be able to spread it over the dough easily and evenly. If the filling is too cold, the dough may tear. If it's too warm, it'll be a bear to roll up.

INGREDIENTS

1 cup (2 sticks) butter, softened

2 cups dark brown sugar

$^1/_4$ cup dark honey

$^1/_4$ cup ground cinnamon

1 tablespoon vanilla extract

DIRECTIONS

1. Mix butter, brown sugar, honey, cinnamon, and vanilla in the bowl of an electric mixer fitted with the paddle attachment.

2. Whip until light and fluffy. Store in an airtight container and keep in the refrigerator for up to 2 weeks. In the freezer, you can store up to 6 months. Thaw completely and fluff up in mixer before using.

Yield: Makes enough to fill 12 cinnamon rolls or two braided cinnamon loaves

Prep time: 5 minutes

Stabilized Whipped Cream

Stabilizing whipped cream with gelatin will allow it to hold its shape longer and can be used as a frosting.

INGREDIENTS

2 ¹/₂ tablespoons water

2 teaspoons unflavored gelatin

1 pint heavy whipping cream

¹/₂ cup powdered sugar

2 teaspoons vanilla extract

DIRECTIONS

1. Refrigerate a bowl for an electric mixer.

2. Add the water and gelatin to a small microwavable bowl. Allow to sit for 3 minutes. Then microwave the gelatin mixture until fully dissolved, just a few seconds. Set aside to cool.

3. Pour the heavy cream, powdered sugar, and vanilla into the refrigerated bowl of an electric mixer fitted with the whisk attachment. Whip on medium until soft peaks begin to form, then mix on low. Drizzle in the gelatin mixture until it mixes fully. Increase the mixer speed to medium, and whip until stiff peaks form.

4. Either pipe or spread onto your dessert. Refrigerate until ready to serve.

Yield: Makes enough to cover one 2-layer 9-inch cake or 8 shortcakes

Prep time: 10 minutes

The Perfect Chocolate Ganache

Because there are so few ingredients, high-quality chocolate is important to ensure an amazing flavor. Rich and velvety, it's the perfect topping to any cake, or even over another icing. Try it over the Flourless Chocolate Cake on page 147. This recipe is a quick method and doesn't require a double boiler.

INGREDIENTS

$2/3$ cup high-quality dark chocolate, chopped

3 tablespoons salted butter

1 teaspoon vanilla extract

DIRECTIONS

1. Add the dark chocolate and butter to a microwave-safe bowl. Microwave for 30-second increments, stirring each time. Add the vanilla and stir until completely smooth.

2. Pour over the cake and spread evenly. Allow ganache to set completely, approximately 3 to 4 hours.

Yield: makes enough to cover one flourless chocolate cake or one bundt cake

Prep time: 10 minutes

Cookies and Bars

Cookies

Homemade cookies take me right back to my childhood. And when they're the perfect, chewy texture made with buttery goodness and love, there's almost nothing that beats them.

The Process of Invention

I will be the first to admit that I was a terrible student in high school. Trapped in a desk all day listening to lectures and taking notes was incredibly challenging when there was so much to discover and create. I spent the days counting down the minutes to my art classes that I'd purposefully scheduled at the end of the day so it seemed more like a reward rather than something for which I would be earning a grade. It helped some, but I still managed to spend my academic classes planning what I'd do after the final bell rang.

A new episode of *Good Eats* would air in the evenings, and if I missed it, I would have to wait for a rerun. I may have spent hours during the day listening to lectures on mitochondria while counting ceiling tiles and passing minutes, but when my hero Alton Brown was discussing mirepoix and the maillard reaction, I sat at the coffee table in our living room fully engaged, frantically scribbling notes on each step and fascinating detail. His confident voice, gloriously animated visual aids, and puppetry made him one of my favorite science teachers.

Then aired the episode about how to manipulate a chocolate chip cookie recipe to create different textures and flavors. Up until then, I had only followed the words on the page in fear that any deviation would result in utter failure. Like many who feared baking, that is what I was taught. Now the food god himself was telling me that even in baking I could make calculated changes to create something new out of something familiar. Food was mad science you could eat. Those words were the permission I needed to courageously cannonball into the deep end of recipe creation. For a sixteen-year-old creative thinker and habitual rule-breaker, that permission was empowering.

Now the food god himself was telling me that even in baking I could make calculated changes to create something new out of something familiar.

Since my mom always kept ingredients for chocolate chip cookies in the house, I began playing with sugar ratios and different kinds of butter. Even the way in which ingredients were incorporated would change the texture and flavor. Each step and ingredient was tasted and scrutinized, tested and retested.

Over the years, thousands of cookies were baked and shared with friends and family. I took them to every gathering,

where I would secretly watch people's reactions and count how long it would take until the plate would be empty. It was only then that the chocolate chunk espresso cookie was deemed the winner. It was chewy and crunchy, sweet but not too sweet, and ever so slightly flavored with espresso to enhance the chocolate without becoming bitter.

Heavy on salted butter and dark brown sugar, eggs whipped in to make them shiny on top, a double helping of good vanilla extract, and high-quality ground espresso were the secrets to an irresistible cookie. It should come as no surprise that this was the first cookie I debuted at Spring Hill Bakery, and it still remains one of our bestselling items to date.

As I grew more confident in my baking, I branched out from testing only chocolate chip cookies to other things, including a year where all I made was spaghetti with varying sauces trying to achieve the ultimate combination. The kitchen became a canvas for culinary creativity, where I could endeavor on new flavor adventures. That one episode and Sir Alton's words became a big part of what empowered me to create without fear and love the process of invention.

Chocolate Chunk Espresso Cookies

While everyone has their own idea about what makes the perfect chocolate chip cookie—cakey, gooey, crisp, or chewy—we can all agree on one thing: chocolate chip cookies are awesome. Heavy on the brown sugar, these definitely fall into the chewy-with-crisp-edges category. The espresso gives them a hint of mocha flavor to complement the dark chocolate.

INGREDIENTS

1 1/4 cups dark brown sugar

1/4 cup white sugar

1 cup (2 sticks) butter, softened

2 large eggs

1 tablespoon vanilla extract

2 1/2 cups all-purpose flour

1 tablespoon ground espresso

3/4 teaspoon baking soda

1/2 teaspoon kosher salt

16 ounces dark chocolate bars, chopped

Yield: 2 dozen cookies

Prep time: 10 minutes

Bake time: 14 minutes

DIRECTIONS

1. Preheat oven to 350 degrees.

2. In the bowl of an electric mixer fitted with the paddle attachment, cream together brown sugar, white sugar, and butter until combined, then beat on high speed until the mixture is light and fluffy.

3. Add eggs and vanilla, then beat until light and fluffy. Scrape bottom of bowl to incorporate all sugar and butter.

4. In separate bowl whisk together flour, espresso, baking soda, and salt. Add to flour mixture, and carefully mix on low until combined.

5. Add chocolate and mix thoroughly.

6. Scoop dough into balls, approximately 12 cookies to a cookie sheet.

7. Bake for 12 to 14 minutes, or until tops of cookies are no longer shiny. Do not overbake, as cookies should be soft and chewy.

8. Allow to cool on pans for approximately 5 minutes, then move to a cooling rack, and allow to cool completely before storing.

Toasted Oat Cranberry Cookies

These are definitely not your grandma's oatmeal cookies. Toasting the oats brings out the wonderfully nutty flavor while the bourbon enhances the spices and brown sugar. The end result is so much warmer and more intense than your average cookie, and you'll find just about any excuse to eat these. In fact, back when we were kids, my mom used to hand one or two of these to us on the way to school when we were running late. So as far as I'm concerned, these are totally breakfast food.

INGREDIENTS

2 ½ cups rolled oats

2 ½ cups all-purpose flour

¾ teaspoon baking soda

¾ teaspoon kosher salt

1 tablespoon ground cinnamon

1 ¼ teaspoons ground nutmeg

1 cup (2 sticks) salted butter, softened

½ cup white sugar

1 ½ cups dark brown sugar

2 large eggs

1 tablespoon vanilla extract

1 tablespoon bourbon (optional)

1 ½ cups dried cranberries

Yield: 2 dozen cookies

Prep time: 10 minutes

Bake time: 14 minutes

DIRECTIONS

1. Preheat oven to 350 degrees.

2. In a large skillet, toast oats over medium heat, just until they become fragrant. Allow to cool.

3. In a large bowl whisk together flour, baking soda, salt, cinnamon, and nutmeg.

4. In the bowl of an electric mixer fitted with the paddle attachment, cream together butter, white sugar, and brown sugar. Beat on high for 2 minutes until light and fluffy.

5. Add eggs one at a time, beating after each addition. Add vanilla and bourbon. Scrape down sides to make sure everything is fully mixed.

6. Add flour mixture and combine. Add oats and cranberries, and mix thoroughly.

7. Using cookie scoop, place cookies 2 to 3 inches apart on a baking sheet.

8. Bake for 10 to 12 minutes. Allow to cool on pans for 5 minutes before transferring them to a cooling rack.

Flourless Peanut Butter Cookies

The magic of a good peanut butter cookie lies in the quality of peanut butter and in how little flour you add. Since this recipe contains no flour, it's more intensely flavored. Creamy or crunchy peanut butter can be used based on your preference. Blending brown and white sugars makes these super chewy, and adding just a hint of vanilla adds a little complexity. Try drizzling them with melted chocolate for an extra treat!

INGREDIENTS

2 cups peanut butter (I like Skippy or Jif)

2 large eggs

1 ½ cups white sugar

½ cup dark brown sugar

1 teaspoon vanilla extract

DIRECTIONS

1. Preheat oven to 350 degrees.

2. Mix together peanut butter, eggs, white sugar, brown sugar, and vanilla in the bowl of an electric mixer just until they come together. Do not overmix, as the texture will become sandy and will not hold together when rolled.

3. Roll into balls, and place 2 to 3 inches apart on an ungreased baking sheet. Press the tops of the cookies with a fork to make a crosshatch pattern.

4. Bake for 10 to 12 minutes. Allow to cool for 10 minutes before moving them to a cooling rack.

Yield: 2 dozen cookies

Prep time: 10 minutes

Bake time: 10 to 12 minutes

Molasses Cookies

Growing up, we knew there was one thing we could always depend on: the copper canister in Gramma's pantry always had molasses cookies in it. It didn't seem to matter what time of year it was, if we stopped by for a quick visit, or even if we showed up unannounced, that magic jar faithfully had cookies stored away, waiting for a hungry passerby.

For Christmas one year, as all of the family began to open presents around the tree, the copper and aluminum jar appeared, well-worn and well-loved, wrapped in a bright new ribbon and heavy with beautifully crackled, fragrant cookies and dried apricots—the perfect pairing. There was a collective gasp as the smell of ginger, cloves, and cinnamon filled the room.

Years before, Gramma and Grampa had moved from their house on Primrose Lane to a smaller, more manageable place. This was the house where the four sisters learned to cook in a kitchen adorned with brass fruit drawer pulls, and where prom escorts and dates would come to sit rigidly in the creaky old rocker and wait for my mother or one of my aunts, much to their dismay and Grampa's delight. It was where we played "hide the thimble," learned how to swim and sew, and listened to Gramma read stories of Raggedy Ann at bedtime. It remained the family headquarters after the nest was empty and served as the gathering place for every holiday and happy event. And it was in that pantry where the copper tin lived.

As the jar was passed around that Christmas in my parents' living room and each person took their first bite, it was as if each of us had stepped back in time to the house on Primrose Lane. We remembered sneaking into the pantry for our favorite cookie. Now the jar held more than just cookies; it held the memories of our childhood too.

From the tears in his eyes, I knew it may have been decades since her passing, yet these cookies had brought back a small piece of her, if only for a moment.

Years later when I opened my baking business so far away from home, I added Gramma's molasses cookies to the menu, hoping others would love them too. A happy phenomenon occurred. Some of my customers told stories of their own connection to the crackly cookies. Some regularly made them for the holidays, using their own family recipes. Others remembered having them as kids. One older gentleman visited my farmers' market booth, took my hand in his, and said, "I just wanted to thank you for making these. I haven't had a molasses cookie like these since my mother passed away."

From the tears in his eyes, I knew it may have been decades since her passing, yet these cookies had brought back a small piece of her, if only for a moment. Someday they will do the same for me.

Hot Toddy Molasses Cookies

Molasses cookies were never-ending in Gramma's house. A copper tin gleamed as you pulled open the pantry door as a sort of beacon of deliciousness. This recipe is a take on her original, mixed with the elements of a hot toddy, making them the ultimate comfort cookies.

INGREDIENTS

1/2 cup (1 stick) salted butter, softened

1 1/2 cups white sugar, plus extra for rolling cookies

1/2 cup firmly packed dark brown sugar

2 large eggs

1/2 cup molasses

1 teaspoon vanilla extract

2 teaspoons honey bourbon

zest from 1 orange

4 cups all-purpose flour

4 teaspoons baking soda

1 teaspoon ground cloves

2 teaspoons ground cinnamon

1 tablespoon crystalized ginger, minced

1 teaspoon kosher salt

Yield: 24 to 36 cookies

Prep time: 10 minutes

Bake time: 10 to 12 minutes

DIRECTIONS

1. Preheat oven to 350 degrees.

2. In the bowl of an electric mixer fitted with the paddle attachment, cream together butter, white sugar, and brown sugar. Texture will be slightly sandy. Using a spatula, scrape the sides and bottom of the bowl to make sure no butter is stuck.

3. Add eggs in one at a time, beating after each addition. Add in molasses, vanilla, bourbon, and orange zest, and beat well. Scrape the bottom of the bowl to make sure all of the ingredients are fully combined.

4. In a separate bowl whisk together flour, baking soda, cloves, cinnamon, ginger, and salt. Add flour mixture into egg mixture and mix on low until a dough forms that can be rolled into a ball.

5. Roll dough into balls the size of a golf ball and roll in white sugar to coat. Place on an ungreased cookie sheet 2 to 3 inches apart. Press down cookies slightly.

6. Bake for 10 to 12 minutes. Once cookies have cooled for 5 minutes, move them to a cooling rack to cool completely.

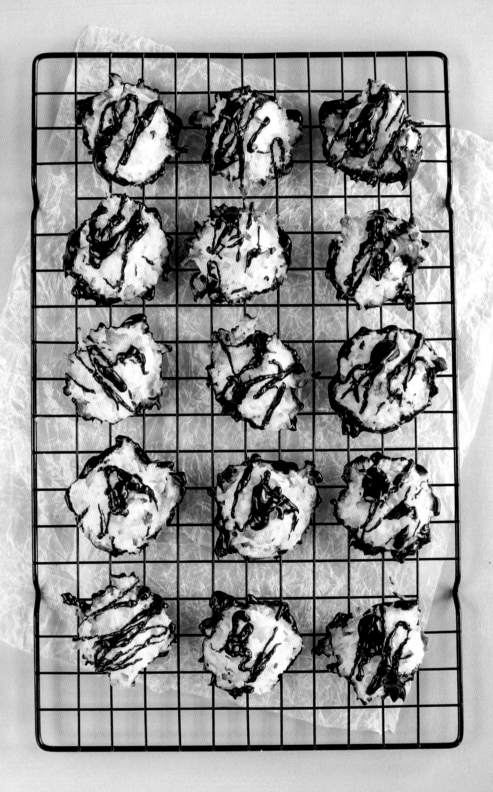

Coconut Drop Cookies

Found stuffed between pages of Great-Grandma's cookbook was this recipe for coconut drop cookies. After making them, I discovered that they were macaroons and decided to add a bit of a chocolate upgrade. If you like your macaroons without chocolate, they're great without it too.

INGREDIENTS

3/4 cup white sugar

3 tablespoons water

1 tablespoon light corn syrup

1 teaspoon kosher salt

14 ounces shredded sweetened coconut

2 large egg whites

2 teaspoons vanilla extract

1/2 cup semisweet chocolate chips

1/4 cup heavy cream

1/2 teaspoon vanilla extract

Yield: 2 dozen cookies

Prep time: 20 minutes

Bake time: 15 to 18 minutes

DIRECTIONS

1. Preheat oven to 350 degrees. Line two baking sheets with parchment paper.

2. In a small saucepan combine sugar, water, corn syrup, and salt. Bring to a boil over medium-high heat. Stir constantly to dissolve sugar. Remove from heat.

3. In a bowl mix together shredded coconut and sugar mixture until completely incorporated. Allow to cool for 20 minutes.

4. Add egg whites and vanilla to a separate bowl. Using a hand mixer, beat until soft peaks form. Gently fold the coconut mixture into the egg whites.

5. Use a cookie scoop to scoop the mixture into mounds on the baking sheets. Space 2 inches apart.

6. Bake 15 to 18 minutes, or until golden brown on top. Allow to cool completely on the baking sheets.

7. In a microwave-safe bowl microwave the chocolate and heavy cream in 10-second intervals, stirring after each interval. Once chocolate is completely melted and smooth, stir in vanilla.

8. Dip the bottoms of each macaroon in chocolate, shaking off excess and returning to parchment to set. Drizzle the tops with more chocolate. Allow chocolate to set.

Chocolate Hazelnut Meringues

While sometimes a little tricky to make, light and airy meringue cookies are like happy little clouds. Flavored with high-quality cocoa powder and hazelnuts, these are reminiscent of a certain highly addictive spread. Be sure to allow them to cool as slowly as possible to achieve the right texture.

INGREDIENTS

- 3/4 cup powdered sugar
- 1 tablespoon cocoa powder
- 1/4 cup hazelnuts
- 3 large egg whites, room temperature
- 1/8 teaspoon kosher salt
- 1/8 teaspoon cream of tartar
- 1/2 cup white sugar
- 1 teaspoon vanilla extract

Yield: 2 dozen cookies

Prep time: 20 minutes

Bake time: 2 to 3 hours

DIRECTIONS

1. Preheat oven to 200 degrees. Line a baking sheet with parchment paper.

2. In a bowl sift together the powdered sugar and cocoa powder. Chop the hazelnuts ultra-fine.

3. In the bowl of an electric mixer fitted with the whisk attachment, beat egg whites, salt, and cream of tartar on low-medium until soft peaks form, approximately 60 seconds. Make sure bowl is incredibly clean or the egg whites will not whip properly.

4. While mixing, add in the white sugar 1 tablespoon at a time. Mix on medium-high until stiff peaks form and mixture is glossy. Beat in vanilla.

5. Remove bowl from mixer, and gently fold in powdered sugar mixture. Fold in hazelnuts.

6. Immediately spoon or pipe mounds of meringue onto prepared baking sheet. Meringue can be placed fairly close together.

7. Place on a low rack in the oven and bake for 2 to 3 hours. Turn off oven and allow to cool overnight. Store in an airtight container for up to 2 weeks.

Vanilla and Cacao Nib Meringue Cookies

If you're a big fan of deep, intense chocolate flavor, these are going to be right up your alley. Ground cocoa bean combined with the sweetness of vanilla create the perfect balance. Bonus? They're gluten-free, and they're so good, you won't even miss the flour.

INGREDIENTS

2 tablespoons cacao nibs, plus more for sprinkling

3/4 cup powdered sugar

3 large egg whites, room temperature

1/8 teaspoon kosher salt

1/8 teaspoon cream of tartar

1/2 cup white sugar

2 teaspoons vanilla extract

Baker's Tip: Make sure it's not a humid or rainy day when making these. They will not bake properly.

Yield: 2 dozen cookies

Prep time: 20 minutes

Bake time: 2 to 3 hours

DIRECTIONS

1. Preheat oven to 200 degrees. Line a baking sheet with parchment paper.

2. Chop the cacao nibs ultra-fine either by hand or in a food processor. In a bowl sift together the powdered sugar and cocoa.

3. In the bowl of an electric mixer fitted with the whisk attachment, beat egg whites, salt, and cream of tartar on low-medium until soft peaks form, approximately 60 seconds. Make sure bowl is incredibly clean and not greasy at all; otherwise, the egg whites will not whip properly.

4. Then add in the white sugar 1 tablespoon at a time while the mixer is running. Mix on medium-high until stiff peaks form and mixture is glossy but not dry. Beat in vanilla.

5. Remove bowl from mixer, and gently fold in powdered sugar mixture. Fold in cacao nibs.

6. Immediately spoon or pipe mounds of meringue onto prepared baking sheet. Meringue doesn't spread much, so they can be placed fairly close together. Sprinkle with additional cacao nibs.

7. Place on a low rack in the oven and bake for 2 to 3 hours. Turn off oven and allow to cool overnight. Store in an airtight container for up to 2 weeks.

Classic Sugar Cookies

A good sugar cookie should taste of butter and be just slightly salty-sweet. Made as a drop cookie, these accomplish just that. They can be customized in a hundred different ways. Snickerdoodle? Roll them in cinnamon and sugar. Sprinkles? Press into each cookie before you bake them. Nuts? Mix them in! Or if you're a purist, they're perfect just as they are.

INGREDIENTS

2 1/2 cups all-purpose flour

1/2 teaspoon baking powder

3/4 teaspoon kosher salt

14 tablespoons butter, softened

2 cups sugar, plus extra sugar for rolling

2 large eggs

2 teaspoons vanilla extract

any fillings or toppings you'd like

Yield: 2 dozen cookies

Prep time: 10 minutes

Bake time: 10 to 12 minutes

DIRECTIONS

1. Preheat oven to 350 degrees and place a rack in the center position of the oven.

2. Whisk together flour, baking powder, and salt in a bowl and set aside.

3. In the bowl of an electric mixer fitted with the paddle attachment, cream together butter and sugar first on low to combine and then on high for 5 minutes, or until light and fluffy. Scrape down the sides of the bowl.

4. Add eggs one at a time, beating together after each addition, and scraping sides of the bowl to make sure mixture is fully combined. Add vanilla and mix on low until combined.

5. Add flour mixture and combine just until you don't see any more flour. Remove bowl from electric mixer, and using scraper, fold a few times, checking for even mixing. Fold in any add-ins (chocolate chips, pretzels, etc.) at this time (up to 1 1/2 cups).

6. Using a cookie scoop to ensure uniformity, make balls out of the cookie dough, and coat in sugar, cinnamon sugar, sprinkles, or whatever you'd like. Place on a cookie sheet 2 to 3 inches apart.

7. Bake for 10 to 12 minutes until edges are slightly browned and crispy. Allow to cool on the tray for 10 minutes before moving them to a cooling rack.

Strawberry Lime Sugar Cookies

These sweet and zesty cookies are what summertime is made of. Freeze-dried strawberries add an intense fruity flavor, and the lime gives them the perfect amount of tartness.

INGREDIENTS

2 ½ cups all-purpose flour

½ teaspoon baking powder

¾ teaspoon kosher salt

14 tablespoons salted butter, softened

2 cups white sugar, plus extra sugar for rolling

2 large eggs

2 teaspoons vanilla extract

zest of 1 lime

1 cup freeze-dried strawberries, crushed

Yield: 2 dozen cookies

Prep time: 10 minutes

Bake time: 12 to 14 minutes

DIRECTIONS

1. Preheat oven to 350 degrees.

2. Whisk together flour, baking powder, and salt.

3. In the bowl of an electric mixer fitted with the paddle attachment, cream together butter and sugar, first on low to combine and then on high until light and fluffy. The color should be almost completely white. Scrape the sides and bottom of the bowl to ensure everything is combined.

4. Add eggs one at a time, beating after each addition. Scrapes sides and bottom of bowl to make sure everything is mixed evenly. Add vanilla and lime, stirring to combine.

5. Add flour mixture and mix just until combined. Crush strawberries into small pieces then add to mixture and combine completely.

6. Using a cookie scoop to ensure uniformity, make balls out of the cookie dough, roll smooth, and then toss in sugar to coat. Place cookies on a baking sheet 2 to 3 inches apart and press down lightly to help with spreading.

7. Bake for 12 to 14 minutes, or until edges are just slightly brown and crispy. Allow to cool on the tray as cookies will be very soft.

Melting Pot Cookies

Starting with a classic chocolate chip cookie, giving it a Tennessee twist, and loading it full of other goodies, this cookie became a symbol of the melting together of different cultures.

INGREDIENTS

1 $1/4$ cups dark brown sugar

$1/4$ cup white sugar

1 cup (2 sticks) butter, softened

2 large eggs

1 tablespoon vanilla extract

1 tablespoon honey bourbon

2 $1/2$ cups all-purpose flour

$3/4$ teaspoon baking soda

$1/2$ teaspoon kosher salt

1 cup chocolate chips

$1/4$ cup white chocolate chips

$1/4$ cup butterscotch chips

$1/4$ cup Heath bar, chopped

$1/4$ cup crushed potato chips

DIRECTIONS

1. Preheat oven to 350 degrees.

2. In the bowl of an electric mixer fitted with the paddle attachment, cream together brown sugar, white sugar, and butter until combined, then beat on high speed until the mixture is light and fluffy.

3. Add eggs, bourbon, and vanilla, then beat until light and fluffy. Scrape bottom of bowl to incorporate all sugar and butter.

4. In a separate bowl whisk together flour, baking soda, and salt. Add to flour mixture, and carefully mix on low until combined.

5. Add chocolate, white chocolate, butterscotch, Heath bar, and potato chips, and mix thoroughly.

6. Scoop dough into balls onto a cookie sheet.

7. Bake for 12 to 14 minutes. Do not overbake, as cookies should be soft and chewy.

8. Allow to cool on pans for approximately 5 minutes, then move to a cooling rack, and allow to cool completely before storing.

Yield: 2 dozen cookies

Prep time: 10 minutes

Bake time: 12 to 14 minutes

Great-Grandma Eva's Lemon Shortbread with Strawberry Icing

Shortbread is one of those recipes we usually associate with Christmas. While this cookie is definitely a holiday staple, I enjoy them year-round. The dough for this recipe is great to make ahead and pull out when you know you'll be having guests. The lemon adds extra zing to this classic cookie. If you're short on time, you can refrigerate the cookies after decorating so the icing will firm up a little bit faster.

INGREDIENTS

1 cup (2 sticks) salted butter, softened

1/2 cup powdered sugar

2 cups all-purpose flour

1/4 teaspoon baking powder

1/4 teaspoon kosher salt

1 teaspoon vanilla extract

1 tablespoon fresh lemon zest

STRAWBERRY BUTTERMILK ICING

1/2 cup freeze-dried strawberries

1 cup powdered sugar, sifted

1/2 teaspoon vanilla extract

4 to 5 tablespoons buttermilk

Yield: 30 to 36 cookies

Prep time: 20 minutes

Bake time: 18 to 20 minutes

DIRECTIONS

1. In a large bowl mix together butter, powdered sugar, flour, baking powder, salt, vanilla, and lemon zest until dough comes together. Form into a disk and wrap tightly with plastic wrap. Refrigerate for 30 minutes or until firm.

2. Preheat oven to 350 degrees.

3. Unwrap dough, sprinkle with flour, and roll between two pieces of parchment paper to 1/4 inch thick. Cut into rectangles. Place on a baking sheet lined with parchment 1 inch apart. Cookies will spread just a little.

4. Bake for 18 to 20 minutes, or until the bottoms are brown. Allow to cool for 10 minutes on baking sheet before moving cookies to a cooking rack. Cool completely.

5. To make the icing, crush freeze-dried strawberries into a fine powder, and mix in a bowl with sifted powdered sugar. Stir in vanilla and 2 tablespoons of buttermilk at a time until consistency is smooth and can be drizzled.

Orange Shortbread Cookies with Chocolate Ganache and Hazelnuts

Like the lemon shortbread, this is a great make-ahead dough you can pull out whenever the craving for a delicious cookie hits you. The orange gives the dough zest, and the chocolate and hazelnuts add wonderful flavor. If you're short on time, you can refrigerate the cookies after decorating so the ganache will firm up a little bit faster.

INGREDIENTS

1 cup (2 sticks) salted butter, softened

$1/2$ cup powdered sugar

1 teaspoon vanilla extract

1 tablespoon fresh orange zest

$1/2$ cup cornstarch

1 cup all-purpose flour

$1/2$ teaspoon kosher salt

GLAZE

$1/2$ cup heavy cream

1 cup dark chocolate, chopped finely

$1/4$ cup hazelnuts, chopped finely

DIRECTIONS

1. In the bowl of an electric mixer fitted with the paddle attachment, cream together butter and sugar until light and fluffy. Scrape down the sides of the bowl, then add vanilla and orange zest and beat again.

2. In a separate bowl sift together cornstarch, flour, and salt.

3. Add flour mixture to the butter mixture $1/2$ cup at a time.

4. Once all the flour has been added, turn out dough onto a large piece of plastic wrap, then form dough into a log approximately 12 inches long. Wrap tightly in plastic wrap, twisting the ends. Refrigerate for 1 hour or until completely firm.

5. Preheat oven to 350 degrees.

6. Unwrap dough, and slice into $1/4$-inch-thick slices. Place on a baking sheet lined with parchment 1 inch apart. Cookies will spread just a little.

RECIPE CONTINUES

Yield: 30 to 36 cookies

Prep time: 20 minutes

Bake time: 15 to 17 minutes

7. Bake for 15 to 17 minutes, or until the bottoms are brown. Allow to cool for 10 minutes on cookie sheet before moving cookies to a cooling rack. Cool completely.

8. To make the glaze, heat cream in a saucepan over medium heat until scalding (do not boil). Add chocolate and allow to stand for 5 minutes. Stir until smooth. Using a fork, drizzle ganache over cookies, and sprinkle with chopped hazelnuts. Alternately, dip cookies halfway in ganache, shaking off extra, and returning to parchment to harden.

Grandma Carol's Russian Tea Cakes

Growing up, Grandmama made these tea cakes every Christmas. As the kid with a major sweet tooth, I used to sneak more than my fair share when we'd go over for presents. Now when I bake these, I love eating them when they're still warm from the oven.

INGREDIENTS

1 cup (2 sticks) butter, softened

2 teaspoons vanilla extract

1/2 cup powdered sugar, sifted

2 1/3 cups all-purpose flour

1/4 teaspoon kosher salt

2/3 cups pecans, finely chopped

powdered sugar for rolling

DIRECTIONS

1. Line two baking sheets with parchment paper.

2. In the bowl of an electric mixer fitted with the paddle attachment, mix together butter, vanilla, and powdered sugar until light and fluffy.

3. Add flour and salt, and mix until dough comes together. Add finely chopped nuts and mix until incorporated. Refrigerate for 1 hour.

4. Preheat oven to 375 degrees.

5. Scoop dough into tablespoon-size balls, roll smooth, and set on the baking sheets. Bake for 8 minutes.

6. Allow to cool just long enough so you can handle them, and then toss cookie balls in powdered sugar until fully coated. Place on a rack to cool. Enjoy within 4 days.

Yield: 3 dozen

Prep time: 15 minutes

Inactive time: 1 hour

Bake time: 8 minutes

Bars

Bars are just as delicious as cookies and are often easier as they don't require the individual placement on a baking sheet, nor is there much worry about what shape they will be, or if they will all run together.

Lemon Bars

I knew when I was creating my lemon bars, I wanted to start with Aunt Glenda's shortbread crust, a super-thick buttery cookie to balance out the tartness of the lemon curd baked on top. This recipe goes together so easily, you'll wonder why you don't make lemon bars all the time. Be sure to use a long piece of parchment so you can carefully lift the bars out of the pan once they're cooled.

CRUST

$\frac{1}{2}$ cup (1 stick) butter, melted

$\frac{1}{4}$ cup powdered sugar

1 cup all-purpose flour

$\frac{1}{8}$ teaspoon kosher salt

FILLING

1 cup white sugar

2 tablespoons all-purpose flour

$\frac{1}{4}$ teaspoon kosher salt

$\frac{1}{2}$ cup fresh lemon juice

2 tablespoons lemon zest

2 large eggs

powdered sugar for dusting

DIRECTIONS

1. Preheat oven to 350 degrees. Grease an 8 x 8-inch pan with nonstick spray, and line with a long piece of parchment.

2. To make the crust, mix butter, powdered sugar, flour, and salt together in a bowl until a smooth dough forms. Press into bottom of pan. Bake for 20 minutes.

3. To make filling, in a bowl whisk together sugar, flour, salt, lemon juice, zest, and eggs until smooth. Pour on top of baked crust, and bake for 20 minutes, or just until firm. Allow to cool 10 minutes before running a knife around the perimeter to make removal easier. Cool completely before removing from pan and cutting.

4. Dust with powdered sugar.

Yield: 16 bars

Prep time: 15 minutes

Bake time: 40 minutes

Bar Snack Blondies

If a brownie wanted to be a chocolate chip cookie, it would take the form of a blondie. Blondies can be loaded up with any number of add-ins, but some of my favorite combinations include the saltiness of peanuts, pretzels, and potato chips combined with dark chocolate. Dark brown sugar makes these cookies extra-chewy with an almost caramel quality about them, making the perfect indulgence.

INGREDIENTS

1 cup (2 sticks) salted butter, melted

1 3/4 cups dark brown sugar

3 large eggs

2 tablespoons vanilla extract

2 1/2 cups all-purpose flour

1/2 teaspoon baking powder

2 teaspoons kosher salt

1/2 cup dark chocolate chips

1/2 cup crushed pretzels

1/2 cup peanuts

1/2 cup crushed wavy potato chips

DIRECTIONS

1. Preheat oven to 350 degrees. Prepare a 9 x 13-inch pan with parchment paper and nonstick cooking spray.

2. In a large bowl stir together the butter and sugar. In a separate bowl whisk eggs and vanilla, then stir into the butter and sugar to combine.

3. In another bowl whisk together flour, baking powder, and salt. Add the flour mixture to the egg mixture and mix well. Fold in the chocolate chips, pretzels, peanuts, and potato chips.

4. Spread the batter into the prepared pan. Top with more chocolate chips, pretzels, peanuts, and potato chips.

5. Bake for 25 to 30 minutes, or until a toothpick comes out clean. Cool, cut into squares, and enjoy!

Yield: 12 large blondies

Prep time: 10 minutes

Bake time: 25 to 30 minutes

Aunt Glenda's Shortbread

I don't know much about Aunt Glenda, but based on her instructions for her shortbread recipe, I can surmise she was a no-nonsense woman who didn't mind getting messy. My kind of woman. The directions below are her exact words that were typed on a notecard. When I make this recipe, I add a teaspoon of vanilla and then drizzle with maple icing and chopped pecans.

INGREDIENTS

1 cup (2 sticks) salted butter

1/2 cup powdered sugar

2 cups all-purpose flour

1/4 teaspoon baking powder

1/4 teaspoon kosher salt

MAPLE ICING

2 cups powdered sugar

1 teaspoon pure maple extract

3 tablespoons milk (more if necessary)

DIRECTIONS

1. Just wash your hands, dump all ingredients into a bowl, and get in there and mix all together until you have a smooth dough.

2. Set oven at 350 degrees. Roll dough 1/4 inch thick on a lightly floured board or between two pieces of wax paper.

3. Cut and put on ungreased cookie sheet.

4. Decorate with anything such as nuts, cherries, or chocolate chips. Bake 20 minutes or until a light straw color. Watch carefully toward the last, because if they brown too much, they lose their flavor.

Yield: 2 dozen

Prep time: 5 minutes

Bake time: 20 minutes

Dark Fudge Hazelnut Brownies

One of life's greatest pleasures is a brownie that is so chocolatey that it teeters on the edge of fudge. These brownies do exactly that.

INGREDIENTS

4 large eggs

1 cup white sugar

1 cup dark brown sugar

1/2 cup all-purpose flour

1 1/4 cup cocoa powder

1/2 teaspoon kosher salt

1 tablespoon vanilla extract

1 cup (2 sticks) butter, melted

1/2 cup chocolate chips

1/4 cup chopped hazelnuts

Gluten-free note: Because this recipe has such a small amount of flour, it can easily be replaced with your favorite gluten-free flour blend.

Yield: 16 brownies

Prep time: 10 minutes

Bake time: 40 to 45 minutes

DIRECTIONS

1. Preheat oven to 325 degrees. Grease a 9 x 9-inch pan, and line with parchment paper.

2. Add eggs to the bowl of an electric mixer fitted with the paddle attachment and beat until frothy. Add white sugar and brown sugar, and beat until light and fluffy.

3. In a separate bowl whisk together flour, cocoa powder, and salt. Slowly add flour mixture to mixer and combine on low. Add vanilla and combine.

4. With mixer on low, slowly add melted butter until completely combined. Add half of the chocolate chips and mix to incorporate.

5. Pour brownie mix into prepared pan and tap on the counter to help distribute evenly. Sprinkle the rest of the chocolate chips and the hazelnuts over the top of the brownies.

6. Bake for 40 minutes, or until a toothpick inserted comes out almost completely clean. A little wet is okay.

7. Allow to cool for 5 to 10 minutes before removing from the pan. Then transfer to a cutting board to slice while they're still warm.

8. Place cut brownies on a cooling rack to cool completely or enjoy warm.

Pies and Tarts

Pies

When just the right crust is paired with a delicious, well-crafted filling, pies—both sweet and savory—can wow any crowd.

Recipes from the Past

When Grandmama Carol passed away, I inherited a giant stack of recipes. Within the stack was a small, well-worn and spattered blue binder with a note in it that said it belonged to my Great-Grandma Eva. Each page was handwritten in black ink or pencil. *The mother lode.* The stories surrounding Eva's baking were the stuff of legends. Pies were her specialty, and Grandmama had once told me that Eva had a Midas touch when it came to the level of perfection she could achieve. She was quite a formidable church lady in a starched apron and pearls, armed with a rolling pin and an oven.

Tucked between every stained page were notecards with even more recipes, some typewritten, others scribbled out as if transcribed while on the phone or maybe while listening to the radio. Rocky Road Frosting. A 170-year-old gingerbread loaf. And a recipe titled Plain Cake that lists nine ingredients and exactly three words of instruction: "mix as given." No pan size, no oven temp, no bake time.

With Eva being somewhat of a da Vinci with a wooden spoon, it didn't completely surprise me to learn that her book of delicious concoctions had been written so cryptically. Like most blue-ribbon home bakers, Eva kept her recipes top secret, and the most stained pages lack critical details. Undoubtedly, those were the most used and inarguably her favorites.

Since Evil Eva passed away in the early 1950s, asking her directly would be impossible. Though if legend has it, she would not have shared anyway. Her methods and techniques were strictly classified. What Eva didn't anticipate was that her great-granddaughter would be a sleuth and twice as stubborn. I was going to make her cake and eat it too, now that I had her sacred texts.

Off to work I went, scouring my vintage cookbooks, all published prior to 1950. *Better Homes & Gardens. Betty Crocker. Good Housekeeping. The American Woman Cookbook.* Anything that would lead me to more information on how to translate Eva's version of the Dead Sea Scrolls. The best part, I figured, was that she wasn't here to tell me I was making her cake wrong or that I didn't use the right frosting. With that sort of freedom, I was able to crack many of her recipes. While I'll never know if my renditions could ever measure up to hers, in some small way, I am regularly able to connect with an ancestor I will never meet and continue her legacy. Her recipes no longer have to lie dormant, unused, unloved, and unappreciated.

Nowadays I find myself wandering antique shops and flea markets, searching for legacies of other great bakers. Old recipe boxes stuffed full of culinary secrets scribbled on splotchy pages. Recipes in beautiful handwriting lovingly scrawled on cotton tablecloths. If I can connect with my own ancestors through food, then I can also discover others through theirs. Was *this* the secret cornbread recipe? Perhaps it was.

Her recipes no longer have to lie dormant, unused, unloved, and unappreciated.

Grandmas have a way of doing that—making food that can never be duplicated by anyone else. There was something special about the way she put the ingredients together, something only her hands could do so precisely that rendered the most perfect creation, often without measuring. Just a scoop of this and a pinch of that. And each time Grandma makes *those* biscuits, *that* pot roast, or *the* cherry pie that

is superior to every other cherry pie ever made, she shares a bit of her magic with her family—magic that cements memories into not just her family's minds but in their hearts and tastebuds too.

It seems every time family recipes are mentioned, someone's memory is sparked with that one amazing thing that their grandmother or mother made. They recall all the times they had it, and suddenly all of the fond memories attached to that one dish come flooding back. Whether it was cookies to console crocodile tears after a scraped knee, or the cheesecake that was dropped on the floor right before serving and then scraped up and eaten anyway, or the icebox rolls that always accompanied every single holiday meal, one bite transported them back to that precious memory, reliving the past so vividly and fondly it almost felt like a hug.

The thing is, even if we don't make those famed biscuits *exactly* the same, the act of making them still brings us closer to our relatives. And if they knew that we were baking their recipes in an effort to preserve that memory and connection—even if those recipes were heavily guarded—I like to believe that somehow, some way, they feel our love.

Great-Grandma Eva's Blue-Ribbon Piecrust

If ever there was a piecrust that broke the rules and still came out flaky and delicious, this is it. No food processor, no grating frozen butter, no refrigerating for a minimum of thirty minutes, and it still comes out great. It's the answer to low-maintenance piecrust. The only change I made was using butter-flavored shortening instead of regular, as it adds a bit more flavor. I'm sure Grandma would have switched too, had it existed in the 1950s.

INGREDIENTS

2 1/4 cups all-purpose flour

1 teaspoon kosher salt

3/4 cup butter-flavored shortening

7 to 8 tablespoons whole milk, cold

Yield: 2 piecrusts

Prep time: 5 minutes

Bake time: 20 minutes

DIRECTIONS

1. Combine flour and salt into a large bowl. Using a pastry cutter, cut shortening into flour until dough resembles pea-size pieces.

2. Drizzle 2 tablespoons of milk at a time into flour mixture, and mix with hands, tossing the ingredients together. The dough will gradually come together. Form dough into a ball and divide in half. Form each piece into a disk and wrap in plastic wrap.

3. To blind bake, roll out one dough ball to 12-inch round, and transfer to 9-inch pie dish. Cut off excess and crimp edge. Using a fork, poke holes in the bottom of the piecrust. Line with parchment paper and fill with pie weights or dry beans. Cover edge of crust with foil or pie collar.

4. Bake crust at 375 degrees for 20 minutes. Then remove foil, beans, and parchment, and bake for another 5 minutes to brown the crust.

Citrus Meringue Pie

A variation on a lemon meringue pie, this recipe's starring roles go to red grapefruits and Cara Cara oranges with just a hint of lemon. While it's less tart than a lemon meringue pie, it still has a bright citrusy flavor that's not too sweet.

INGREDIENTS

Great-Grandma Eva's Blue-Ribbon Piecrust (page 219)

5 large eggs

1 1/4 cups white sugar, divided

2 cups water

6 tablespoons cornstarch

pinch of salt

4 tablespoons (1/4 stick) butter, softened

1/4 cup fresh grapefruit juice

1/4 cup fresh Cara Cara orange juice

2 tablespoons lemon zest

1 teaspoon lemon juice

DIRECTIONS

1. Preheat oven to 350 degrees.

2. Make the piecrust recipe on page 219. Using half of the dough, line a 9-inch pie pan with dough and crimp the edges. Blind bake for 20 minutes and allow to cool.

3. To make the filling, separate egg yolks and whites. In a medium bowl beat the egg yolks well and set aside.

4. In a medium saucepan combine 1 cup of sugar, water, cornstarch, and pinch of salt. Stir constantly over medium-low heat until mixture comes to a slow boil. Continue to stir until mixture becomes thick. Remove from heat and add a little of this mixture to the egg yolks at a time, whisking vigorously. When approximately 1 cup has been whisked into the yolks, return egg yolk mixture to saucepan, and whisk together on low heat for another 2 minutes.

5. Remove from heat and stir in 1 tablespoon of butter at a time until smooth. Then add grapefruit and orange juice and zest. Stir until smooth. Cover with plastic wrap so a skin doesn't form on the top of the filling and allow to cool to room temperature.

RECIPE CONTINUES

Yield: 9-inch pie

Prep time: 40 minutes

Bake time: 45 minutes

6. Pour into crust, making sure not to overfill.

7. To make meringue, in the bowl of an electric mixer fitted with the whisk attachment, combine egg whites, a pinch of salt, and lemon juice. Whip on high until soft peaks form, and then very gradually add remaining 1/4 cup of sugar. Continue with mixer on high until stiff peaks form. Transfer meringue to pastry bag, and pipe on top of lemon filling, sealing the edges to prevent shrinking.

8. Bake at 325 degrees for 20 to 25 minutes until meringue is golden brown.

9. Cool pie thoroughly before serving.

Mixed Berry Key Lime Pie

One of my favorite things about a Key lime pie—aside from the fact that it's Key lime pie—is that you can add just about any other fruit to it and it makes it that much more awesome. Another great thing about it is that the graham cracker crust can easily be switched out for a gluten-free cracker, cookie, pretzel, or any combination of those three, and you still get a crazy-good pie. For my version, I've substituted crushed pretzels for a third of the crust, Greek yogurt instead of sour cream, and marbled mixed-berry puree into the filling before baking to give it a little extra.

MIXED BERRY PUREE

1/2 cup frozen mixed berries

1 tablespoon white sugar

1/4 cup water

1 tablespoon cornstarch

PIECRUST

1 cup fine graham cracker crumbs

1/2 cup fine pretzel crumbs

5 tablespoons butter, melted

1/4 cup white sugar

1 tablespoon brown sugar

PIE FILLING

28 ounces sweetened condensed milk

1/2 cup Greek yogurt

3/4 cup lime juice

zest of two limes

DIRECTIONS

1. To make the puree, combine the fruit, sugar, and water in a saucepan, and cook on medium-low until the berries break down, stirring often. Mash the fruit as it cooks. Sprinkle in the cornstarch and stir until thickened. Set aside to cool.

2. To make crust, preheat oven to 350 degrees. Place graham cracker crumbs and pretzel crumbs together in a bowl. Add the melted butter, white sugar, and brown sugar, and stir together until the butter is evenly distributed. Firmly press mixture into the bottom and sides of a 9-inch pie pan using the bottom of a measuring cup. Bake crust for 8 minutes. Allow to cool for approximately 30 minutes.

3. To make filling, whisk together sweetened condensed milk, Greek yogurt, lime juice, and lime zest. Pour into piecrust and spread smooth. Drizzle some of the berry puree over the top of the lime filling, and swirl using a toothpick or skewer.

RECIPE CONTINUES

Yield: 1 pie

Prep time: 30 minutes

Bake time: 18 minutes

Inactive: 2 hours

4. Bake at 350 for 10 minutes. Allow to cool for 10 minutes, and then chill in the refrigerator for a minimum of 2 hours.

5. Serve with whipped cream (page 170) and lime zest for garnish.

Mom's Apple Pie

It's not a holiday without Mom's apple pie. Packed full of tart Granny Smith apples and spices, it's still one of my favorite pies ever. Mixing white and brown sugars make it extra tasty. I've made different variations over the years, adding other fruits or a shot of bourbon, but there's nothing quite like the original, tried and true.

INGREDIENTS

Great-Grandma Eva's Blue-Ribbon Piecrust (page 219)

5 to 7 Granny Smith apples

1 teaspoon lemon juice

2 tablespoons all-purpose flour

3/4 cup white sugar

1/4 cup brown sugar

1/8 teaspoon kosher salt

2 teaspoons ground cinnamon

1/2 teaspoon ground nutmeg

2 tablespoons butter

DIRECTIONS

1. Preheat oven to 400 degrees and place a rack in the center position of the oven.

2. Prepare piecrust on page 219, and divide in half, with one half slightly larger than the other. Roll the larger dough to 12 inches in diameter, and line a 9-inch pie pan. Don't trim. Wrap the smaller dough in plastic wrap.

3. Peel and core the apples. Cut into 1/4-inch slices, and place in a large bowl. Toss with lemon juice. Then add flour, white sugar, brown sugar, salt, cinnamon, and nutmeg, and toss again. Pour apples into piecrust.

4. Roll out top crust to fit pie, cut steam holes, and roll the dough over the rolling pin to help place crust over the pie. Seal the two crusts together with a little bit of water and crimp the crust.

5. Bake for 50 minutes. If the crust begins to brown too much, cover with foil.

6. Allow pie to cool completely so pie filling will set.

Yield: One 9-inch pie

Prep time: 30 minutes

Bake time: 50 minutes

Blueberry Crostata

Crostatas are pie's low-maintenance cousin. In fact, given the choice of making an entire pie or a series of crostatas, I tend to go with the latter because they don't have to be perfect. It's usually better when they're not because they're meant to be rustic. This blueberry crostata uses fresh berries; however, you can use frozen as well.

INGREDIENTS

Great-Grandma Eva's Blue-Ribbon Piecrust (page 219)

1 large egg

1 tablespoon water

2 cups fresh blueberries

1/3 cup white sugar

2 teaspoons lemon zest

1 1/2 teaspoons fresh lemon juice

2 tablespoons cornstarch

1 tablespoon butter

1 tablespoon sanding sugar (or turbinado sugar)

DIRECTIONS

1. Preheat oven to 425 degrees.

2. Make piecrust recipe on page 219. Using half the recipe, roll into a 12-inch round, and transfer to a sheet pan lined with parchment.

3. In a small bowl whisk together the egg and water, making an egg wash.

4. In a bowl toss together blueberries, sugar, lemon zest, lemon juice, and cornstarch. Pour berries into the middle of the piecrust. Spread out a little, leaving 2 to 3 inches of crust around the edges. Crumble the butter over the berries. Begin folding the crust over the blueberries, using the egg wash to seal as you go. Once all of the crust is folded up, brush the outside of the piecrust with egg wash. Sprinkle crust with sanding sugar.

5. Bake crostata 23 to 25 minutes, or until crust is golden brown.

6. Allow to cool before moving to a serving tray. Best served with vanilla ice cream!

Yield: one 9-inch crostata

Prep time: 15 minutes

Bake time: 25 minutes

Cherry Almond Crostata

Cherries have such a short season in spring, so take advantage of these incredibly delicious fruits while they're available. For this recipe, I like to mix a few different kinds of cherries, depending on what I can find. Mixing tart with sweet will give a greater depth of flavor in this low-maintenance almost-pie.

INGREDIENTS

Great-Grandma Eva's Blue-Ribbon Piecrust (page 219)

1 large egg

1 tablespoon water

2 cup fresh cherries, pitted and halved

1/4 cup sliced almonds

1/3 cup white sugar

2 teaspoons orange zest

1 1/2 teaspoons fresh orange juice

2 tablespoons cornstarch

1 tablespoon butter

1 tablespoon sanding sugar (or turbinado sugar)

DIRECTIONS

1. Preheat oven to 425 degrees.

2. Make piecrust recipe on page 219. Using half the recipe, roll into a 12-inch round, and transfer to a sheet pan lined with parchment.

3. Whisk together the egg and water, making an egg wash.

4. In a large bowl toss together cherries, almonds, sugar, orange zest, orange juice, and cornstarch. Pour cherries into the middle of the piecrust. Spread out a little, leaving 2 to 3 inches of crust around the edges. Crumble the butter over the cherries. Begin folding the crust over the cherries, using the egg wash to seal as you go. Once all of the crust is folded up, brush the outside of the piecrust with egg wash. Sprinkle crust with sanding sugar.

5. Bake crostata 23 to 25 minutes, or until crust is golden brown.

6. Allow to cool before moving to a serving tray. Best served with ice cream.

Yield: 1 crostata

Prep time: 15 minutes

Bake time: 25 minutes

Banana Cream Pie

Starting with a rich vanilla pudding layered with bananas and topped with whipped cream, banana cream pie was one of Great-Grandma's most-made recipes.

PUDDING

Great-Grandma Eva's
   Blue-Ribbon Piecrust
   (page 219)

1 cup white sugar

3 tablespoons butter

1 1/2 cups whole milk

6 tablespoons cornstarch

2 egg yolks, beaten

1 tablespoon vanilla extract

1/8 teaspoon cinnamon

1/8 teaspoon kosher salt

3 ripe bananas, sliced

WHIPPED CREAM

2 cups heavy cream

3 tablespoons powdered sugar

1 teaspoon vanilla extract

Yield: 10-inch pie

Prep time: 20 minutes

Bake time: 25 minutes (piecrust)

Inactive time: 2 hours

DIRECTIONS

1. Make piecrust on page 219 and blind bake. Allow to cool.

2. In a saucepan over medium heat, mix together sugar and butter until sugar has melted. Add milk and cornstarch, and whisk together.

3. Increase heat to medium-high and bring to a boil, stirring constantly. Boil 1 minute until thick.

4. Add a little at a time to beaten egg yolks while whisking vigorously. Once approximately 1 cup has been added, transfer egg yolk mixture back into saucepan. Whisk together and bring to a boil for 1 minute. Add vanilla and cinnamon and combine. Pour mixture into a bowl and cover the surface of pudding with plastic wrap so it doesn't form a skin. Refrigerate until the mixture is room temperature.

5. To assemble, layer half of the bananas into piecrust, and cover with a layer of pudding. Layer remaining bananas, and cover with the rest of the pudding. Refrigerate for 2 hours.

6. To make whipped cream, add heavy cream, powdered sugar, and vanilla to a large bowl, and beat with a hand mixer until stiff peaks form. Cover the top of the pie with whipped cream and serve.

Blackberries

H ere," Gramma said, handing each of us a bucket. "Come with me."

My little brother, Bryan, and I eagerly put on our boots and followed her. The excitement in her voice meant adventure was nearby, and buckets meant treasures. We plodded along the bank of the lazy river, wondering what Gramma had in store for us. It was cool for July in Sonoma County. Giant pillowy clouds had blown in from the California coast and floated in the deep blue sky above the tall pines. It felt like we were camping in a Bob Ross painting. Soon, we came upon the bridge at the entrance to the Thousand Trails campground.

"Blackberries!" she exclaimed, approaching an overgrown hedge speckled with fruit. "Only pick the dark ones. The red ones aren't ready yet." Everything was a teaching moment with Gramma. "Be careful of the prickers. Only touch the fruit." By that time I'd already learned that the bush could bite back.

I remember thinking it was so funny that we could pick berries in the wild without needing to ask anyone permission. Wouldn't we get into trouble? I picked cautiously and quickly just in case the park ranger came to protest. Better eat a few so I wouldn't have to give them back. I wasn't sure what the punishment would've been, but luckily, we never found out.

She glanced at our faces and laughed. "I think you've eaten more than you've got in your bucket!"

I may have eaten two for every one that made it into my pail. The bushes were so full of fruit that it didn't matter how many we'd eaten. The more we picked, the more fruit there seemed to be. I'd never had berries so delicious before. These were bigger than my thumbs and twice as sweet.

> By their excitement, you'd have thought she'd revealed buckets of gold instead of fruit.

Once our buckets and bellies were full, we began the short trek back to camp, our journey made longer with the heavy pails. Gramma carried Bryan's bucket as he ran ahead, collecting rocks and sticks with his purple hands and stuffing them into his pockets. At six years old, with blond hair and the energy of a lightning bolt, he might've been one slingshot shy of being the real Dennis the Menace.

"Oh dear. Your mother won't be too pleased to empty his pockets later," Gramma said. She laughed and shook her head. I smiled to myself, knowing she was right.

Camping trips always included extended family. There were never less than five RVs in our caravan, and everyone always pitched in to help with meals.

Gramma held up her two buckets and announced, "Blackberries!"

By their excitement, you'd have thought she'd revealed buckets of gold instead of fruit. All of the women sprung up from their lawn chairs and card games, disappeared into their campers for a moment, and emerged with rolling pins, pie pans, and bags of ingredients. Then we all me made our way to Gramma's motorhome. It always amazed me that, even while on vacation, everyone was at the ready for impromptu baking sessions, even in the July heat.

Once inside, every surface was transformed into a workstation, and jobs were assigned. In that tiny space, we somehow created an assembly line. Gramma and Annette made dough at the small counter while Mom and I sat in the front seats and sorted berries, keeping our faces swiveled to the party. Gramma's nieces rolled out crusts at the kitchenette while their daughters filled them in their laps. At the end of the rotation, the pies made it back to the counter to be topped. I can't remember who came up with the idea, but someone had used a piping tip to stamp blackberry patterns into the crusts before they were set on top of those mountains of berries and sugar. I'd never seen such an intricate design on a pie before. I watched intently as Gramma and Annette expertly crimped the crusts into perfect waves, sealing all that goodness inside. Their hands moved so effortlessly over the dough; it was as if they'd been born with the ability to make perfect pies. I prayed the trait was hereditary.

Community pie marathons should still be a thing.

One by one the pies were paraded to every available oven. As a shy nine-year-old, I sat and listened to the stories they told. They recounted other pie-making adventures and memories of young adulthood, exchanging ideas and tips for creating new pies. It was complete mayhem and filled with so much joy.

Now, when I buy blackberries, it reminds me of that spontaneous day and all the other days like it. I remember the organized chaos and laughter that came with creating that beautiful mess together. Community pie marathons should still be a thing.

I created the following recipe in honor of that day. I'm not sure who has the original, or if there ever was one. Pies were so common in our family that the recipe may have never been written down. If there's one thing that should be remembered, it's to find the biggest, plumpest, sweetest blackberries. Dark ones, because the red ones aren't ready yet.

Blackberry Pie

Whether you visit a farmers' market or grow them yourself, there's nothing better than perfectly ripe berries to make this pie it's most delicious. Using lime zest instead of lemon gives this pie a twist.

INGREDIENTS

6 cups ripe blackberries (see note for frozen)

Great-Grandma Eva's Blue-Ribbon Piecrust (page 219)

3/4 cup white sugar

1/4 cup cornstarch

1/2 teaspoon fresh lime zest

1 large egg

2 tablespoons water

turbinado or sanding sugar for top

Yield: 1 pie

Prep time: 20 minutes

Bake time: 50 to 60 minutes

DIRECTIONS

1. Preheat oven to 350 degrees.

2. Clean blackberries of any stems, leaves, or debris and rinse. Lay on paper towels to dry.

3. Make piecrust on page 219, and split into two balls, one slightly bigger than the other. Press larger one into a round disk and cover the smaller in plastic wrap and set aside.

4. Roll out the larger piecrust to a 12-inch diameter to fit a 9-inch pie dish. Roll the dough around the rolling pin to transfer to pie dish. Don't trim the edges, as this will be used to seal the lattice in place.

5. In a bowl toss berries in sugar, cornstarch, and lime zest. Carefully pour berries into piecrust.

6. Whisk egg and water together to create an egg wash.

7. Roll out second piecrust to approximately 10 inches and cut into 1-inch-wide strips. Weave into a lattice pattern, and trim off extra length. Seal ends to bottom crust, and crimp bottom crust.

8. Brush lattice with egg wash, and sprinkle with sanding sugar.

9. Bake for 30 minutes with the crust covered with foil, and then for an additional 20 minutes uncovered so the crust will brown.

10. Allow pie to cool on a rack for at least 2 hours for filling to set.

Mini Peach Cobblers with Buttermilk Biscuits

My favorite way to make a cobbler is to pile buttermilk biscuits on top. As they bake, they soak up all of the fruit juices while staying crispy on top. Whether you're serving this individually in ramekins or in a cast-iron skillet, whatever you do, don't forget a big scoop of vanilla ice cream.

INGREDIENTS

6 to 7 large peaches, pitted and sliced

$1/3$ cup white sugar

$1/3$ cup brown sugar

3 tablespoons cornstarch

1 tablespoon lemon juice

$1/4$ teaspoon ground cinnamon

$1/8$ teaspoon ground nutmeg

$1/2$ teaspoon kosher salt

Buttermilk Biscuit recipe (page 104)

buttermilk

DIRECTIONS

1. Preheat oven to 375 degrees.

2. Toss peaches, white sugar, brown sugar, cornstarch, lemon juice, cinnamon, nutmeg, and salt together in a bowl, and divide evenly between 6 medium-size ramekins or in a seasoned 10-inch cast-iron skillet.

3. Make the biscuit dough (page 104). Using a large round biscuit cutter, cut out the biscuits, and place one in each of the ramekins on top of the peaches. If you're baking in the skillet, place the biscuits on top of the peaches in the skillet. Brush biscuits with buttermilk.

4. Place all of the ramekins on a baking sheet, and transfer to the oven and bake them for 60 to 70 minutes, until golden brown and bubbly. Skillet will bake for roughly the same amount of time.

5. Allow to cool for approximately 30 minutes and serve with ice cream.

Yield: Six 14-ounce ramekins

Prep time: 15 minutes

Bake time: 60 to 70 minutes

Tarts

Tarts differ from pies in that they are typically made with a firmer, thicker crust that can stand alone without support from the pan it's baked in. Whether savory or sweet, tarts have a much firmer filling, and with their open tops, they can be beautifully decorated once the filling has set.

Mini Lemon Meringue Tarts

Whenever there's an opportunity to bake individual desserts for guests, I always jump on it. There's something about a personal-size version that feels extra-special. In this take on a lemon meringue pie, we start with a graham cracker crust pressed into the bottom of a ramekin, then finish by layering on lemon filling and piping meringue on top.

GRAHAM CRACKER CRUST

1 cup fine graham cracker crumbs

½ cup finely crushed pretzels

5 tablespoons butter, melted

¼ cup white sugar

1 tablespoon brown sugar

FILLING

5 large eggs

1 ¼ cups white sugar, divided

2 cups water

6 tablespoons cornstarch

salt

4 tablespoons (½ stick) butter, softened

½ cup fresh lemon juice

2 tablespoons lemon zest

DIRECTIONS

1. Preheat oven to 350 degrees.

2. Make graham cracker crust by mixing together in a bowl graham cracker crumbs, crushed pretzels, melted butter, white sugar, and brown sugar until the texture is sandy but holds together when you squeeze it. Firmly press equal amounts into the bottoms of 5-ounce ramekins. Place all the ramekins on a baking sheet and bake for 7 to 8 minutes.

3. To make filling, separate egg yolks and whites. In a medium bowl beat the egg yolks well and set aside.

4. In a medium saucepan combine 1 cup of sugar, water, cornstarch, and a pinch of salt. Stir constantly over medium-low heat until mixture comes to a slow boil. Continue to stir until mixture thickens.

5. Remove from heat and add a little of this mixture to the egg yolks at a time, whisking vigorously. When approximately 1 cup has been whisked into the yolks, return egg yolk mixture to saucepan, and whisk together on low heat for another 2 minutes.

RECIPE CONTINUES

6. Remove from heat and stir in 1 tablespoon of butter at a time until smooth. Then add lemon juice and zest and stir until smooth.

7. Pour into crusts, making sure not to overfill.

8. To make meringue, in the bowl of an electric mixer with the whisk attachment, combine egg whites, a pinch of salt, and 1 teaspoon of lemon juice. Whip on high until soft peaks form, and then very gradually add $\frac{1}{4}$ cup of sugar. Continue with mixer on high until stiff peaks form. Transfer meringue to a pastry bag, and pipe on top of lemon filling, sealing the edges to prevent shrinking.

9. Bake at 325 degrees for 20 to 25 minutes until meringue is golden brown.

10. Cool pies thoroughly in the fridge before serving.

Yield: 6 mini tarts

Prep time: 40 minutes

Bake time: 40 minutes

Fig Honey Mascarpone Tart

Blending together the sweet and tart flavors of both the mascarpone and fig give this dessert a sophisticated edge. Fresh figs can be found in many different varieties, depending on what region you're in and what's available to you. Some will taste sweeter while others will be more tart.

PIECRUST

1 1/2 cups fine graham cracker crumbs

5 tablespoons butter, melted

1/4 cup white sugar

1 tablespoon brown sugar

FILLING

16 ounces mascarpone, softened

1/2 cup white sugar

1 teaspoon vanilla extract

2 tablespoons clover honey, plus additional for drizzling

green figs, quartered

pistachios, crushed

DIRECTIONS

1. To make crust, preheat oven to 350 degrees. In a bowl add graham cracker crumbs, melted butter, white sugar, and brown sugar, and stir together until the butter is evenly distributed. Firmly press mixture into the bottom and sides of a 9-inch tart pan using the bottom of a measuring cup. Bake crust for 8 minutes. Allow to cool completely.

2. To make filling, using either an electric mixer or with a hand mixer, beat mascarpone until completely smooth. Add sugar, vanilla, and honey, and mix until fully combined. Pour filling into cooled crust, and spread evenly with a spatula. Arrange the cut figs on top of the cream, cover with plastic wrap, and refrigerate for 2 to 3 hours before serving.

3. Right before serving, drizzle a little honey over the figs, and sprinkle on the pistachios as a garnish.

Yield: 1 tart

Prep time: 20 minutes

Bake time: 10 minutes

Inactive time: 2 to 3 hours

Apple Cranberry Spice Tart

It's no secret that Thanksgiving is my favorite holiday. In fact, Christmas music is forbidden until the Friday after, just so we can give the holiday its due. This tart is like Thanksgiving in dessert form and regularly makes an appearance on our holiday table. Mixing tart and sweet apples creates more complexity of flavor. Serve this with vanilla ice cream, or with my favorite, butter pecan.

INGREDIENTS

Great-Grandma Eva's Blue-Ribbon Piecrust (half recipe) (page 219)

2 gala or fuji apples, peeled and cored

2 Golden Delicious apples, peeled and cored

2 tablespoons lemon juice

1/4 cup white sugar

1/2 cup brown sugar

zest of 1 orange

2 tablespoons all-purpose flour

1 teaspoon ground cinnamon

1/4 teaspoon ground allspice

1/4 teaspoon ground ginger

1/4 teaspoon ground nutmeg

1/8 teaspoon ground cloves

pinch kosher salt

1 1/2 cups cranberries

DIRECTIONS

1. Preheat oven to 375 degrees.

2. Make piecrust on page 219. Line a 9-inch tart pan with piecrust. Trim and prick the bottom of the piecrust with a fork to prevent bubbling.

3. Slice the peeled and cored apples 1/8 inch thick, and fan them out in the bottom of the crust. Brush with lemon juice to prevent browning.

4. In a bowl mix together white sugar, brown sugar, orange zest, flour, cinnamon, allspice, ginger, nutmeg, cloves, and salt. Toss the cranberries in the sugar and spice mixture, and gently press between the apples, sprinkling the rest of the sugar mixture over the top.

5. Bake pie for approximately 1 hour, or until the apples are soft and the crust is browned. Remove from the oven and allow to cool on a cooling rack. Serve with ice cream.

Yield: One 9-inch tart

Prep time: 20 minutes

Bake time: 1 hour

Raspberry Cheesecake Tart

An ode to summer, fresh raspberries top this no-bake cream cheese tart. With a hint of lemon, this cool dessert is light and refreshing. As with all of the pies and tarts with a cracker crust, you can easily make this gluten-free by substituting your favorite gluten-free cookie or cracker.

PIECRUST

- 1 1/2 cups fine graham cracker crumbs
- 5 tablespoons butter, melted
- 1/4 cup white sugar
- 1 tablespoon brown sugar

FILLING

- 2 (8-ounce) packages cream cheese, softened
- 1/2 cup white sugar
- 1 teaspoon vanilla extract
- 2 tablespoons clover honey
- 1 teaspoon lemon zest
- 1 pint raspberries
- powdered sugar

DIRECTIONS

1. To make crust, preheat oven to 350 degrees. Place graham crackers crumbs in a bowl and add the melted butter, white sugar, and brown sugar. Stir together until the butter is evenly distributed. Firmly press mixture into the bottom and sides of a 9-inch tart pan using the bottom of a measuring cup. Bake crust for 8 minutes. Allow to cool completely

2. To make filling, using either an electric mixer or with a hand mixer, beat cream cheese until completely smooth. Add sugar, vanilla, honey, and lemon zest, and mix until fully combined. Pour filling into cooled crust and spread evenly with a spatula. Arrange the raspberries on top of the cream, cover with plastic wrap, and refrigerate for 2 to 3 hours before serving. Right before serving, sprinkle with powdered sugar.

Yield: 1 tart

Prep time: 20 minutes

Bake time: 10 minutes

Inactive time: 2 to 3 hours

Chocolate Turtle Tart

Trading a typical graham cracker crust for one made of chocolate and potato chips adds an unexpected twist to this rich chocolate tart. Adding homemade caramel and pecans over the top makes this truly decadent. The chocolate crackers can be substituted to make a gluten-free version.

PIECRUST

3/4 cup crushed chocolate crackers

1/4 cup crushed potato chips

5 tablespoons butter, melted

1/3 cup white sugar

FILLING

1 1/4 cups heavy cream

9 ounces semisweet chocolate, chopped

2 large eggs

2 teaspoons vanilla extract

1/4 teaspoon kosher salt

CARAMEL

1 cup white sugar

1/2 cup (1 stick) butter, softened

1/3 cup heavy cream

1 teaspoon kosher salt

1/2 cup chopped pecans

DIRECTIONS

1. Preheat oven to 350 degrees.

2. To make crust, add chocolate crackers crumbs and crushed potato chips to a bowl, and mix with butter and sugar. Press into a 9-inch fluted tart pan and bake for 8 minutes. Allow to cool.

3. To make filling, heat heavy cream in a saucepan just until it starts to boil. Remove from heat and add the semisweet chocolate. Allow to stand for 5 minutes, and then stir until smooth. Cool for 15 minutes.

4. In a bowl whisk together eggs, vanilla, and salt. Add cooled chocolate mixture and mix until smooth. Pour filling into cooled crust and bake until filling is set but still wobbly in the center, approximately 20 minutes. Cool completely in the pan on a cooling rack.

5. To make caramel, in a heavy saucepan over medium-low heat, heat the sugar until completely melted, swirling every 15 to 20 seconds. The sugar will become clumpy as it melts. Do not walk away from the pan as it will burn quickly if left too long.

RECIPE CONTINUES

Yield: One 9-inch tart

Prep time: 40 minutes

Bake time: 20 minutes

6. Once melted, remove from heat and immediately stir in butter until smooth. Sugar will bubble a lot during this process. Then add in heavy cream and salt and stir until smooth. Allow to cool completely before using.

7. Drizzle caramel over the tart and sprinkle with chopped pecans.

Acknowledgments

An enormous *thank you* to all of my customers over the years. It has been an honor to serve you through the bakery, through classes, and now through this book. None of it would have been possible without your support and love.

To my husband, Corey, thank you for believing in me before I believed in myself. Your encouragement, pep talks, kind critiques, partnership, and enduring patience are everything. Thank you for being the Desi to my Lucy. You are the actual best.

To my most amazing daughter, Eva Mae, for your heart, your incredible eye for detail, and for being a sounding board when I needed another set of eyes and a hug. You will always be my greatest joy.

To my family for instilling the love of cooking and baking for others. It was surely the best foundation I could have.

To my friends who taste-tested so many things, for your loving critiques, and for midnight pie feasts. You are all the best.

To the absolutely wonderful Mignon Francois, thank you for your friendship, kindness, blessing, and part in this. You are such a joy and light.

To my recipe tester, Matt O'Roark, for your thoroughness and insight. Thank you for your thoughtful feedback.

To the unbelievably talented team at HarperCollins Christian—especially my editors, Bonnie Honeycutt and Adria Haley, and my book designer, Tiffany Forrester—for all of your hard work on this project. You are the absolute dream team. Thank you for believing in this project and completely knocking it out of the park. I am so blessed to work with you and I'll never be able to thank you enough for everything you've done.

To my antique friends at 2 Storeys, Carter's Creek Station Antiques, Bleu 32, and Spring Hill Antique Mall for hunting down and contributing beautiful photo props to help bring personality and character to this book. Special thanks to Carol and Bubba for such great conversation and encouragement.

And finally, many dear friends, for your encouragement and love along the way: Arica and Kevin Robinson, Alicia Fitts, Chuck Byrn, Katrina and Gerald Beckham, Sherri Hildreth (for friendship and the most amazing hair ever), Kirstin Hunt, Keith and Echan Groves, Josh Merrill (for keeping me caffeinated at Legacy Coffee), and every other person I'm sure I'm forgetting.

About the Author

Sarah Gonzalez moved halfway across the country to Spring Hill, Tennessee, and soon began to spend a lot of time baking and cooking for new friends. Just six months after putting down new roots, she began baking for the farmer's market. Having grown up with a family whose get-togethers were centered around baking, cooking, and canning, Sarah began making food to help ease homesickness for herself and the many other transplants in the area. Without any formal training, Sarah turned her lifelong love of creating food and nurturing people into a full-fledged bakery. She started in her home kitchen and eventually landed in a brick-and-mortar store in the middle of town. Spring Hill Bakery now serves as an online baking school, teaching people to create delicious food, how to serve it, and how to feed people. It's a mixture of handmade breads, incredible desserts, and comforting classics. She teaches the how and the why behind baking, giving even beginning bakers the confidence to create so that even more people are being fed—heart, bellies, and soul.

To learn more about classes or more delicious recipes, and keep up with new projects Sarah is cooking up, please visit either breadladyskitchen.com or springhillbakery.com. You can also follow her on Instagram at @breadladyskitchen and @springhillbakery.